INDIAN WOMEN'S POETRY

A STUDY IN SCHIZOPHRENIC EXPERIENCE

INDIAN WOMEN'S POETRY

A STUDY IN SCHIZOPHRENIC EXPERIENCE

Tanu Gupta

prestigebooks
INTERNATIONAL PUBLISHING

Published by
Prestige Books International
New Delhi 110 060
Ph. 9818755529
email: prestigebooks@gmail.com
website: asiabookclub.com

Associate Office
60/29-45 Parramatta Road,
Concord, NSW 2137
Australia

ISBN: 81-7851-090-1

Printed at Chaman Offset Press, New Delhi 110 002

Contents

for

My loving

Nonu and Cutu

Preface

Feminism which has ruled the literary canon in the West for a number of decades is now spreading to Third World like wildfire. Indian women, too, under the influence of feminist ideologies, awoke to their pathetic plight, and began to express their assertion and independence. But this essential process of self-definition is complicated by all those patriarchal prescriptions that intervene between what women want to be and what they are supposed to be, and ultimately results in a dichotomy between their feminist desires on one side and their social roles on the other, leading to their schizophrenic existence.

A similar conflicting aspect resulting in schizophrenia has been observed in the poetry of contemporary Indian English women poets and the aim of the present study is to explore this tendency in the poetry of Mamta Kalia, Gauri Deshpande, Suniti Namjoshi, Lalitha Venkateswaran, Eunice de Souza, Sunita Jain and Debjani Chatterjee. The insights from psychoanalytical feminist perspectives have been used to analyze the schizophrenic existence of these poets and the present study has been broadly classified in five chapters:

"Between Conformity and Rebellion: A Brief Survey of Contemporary Indian Women's Poetry" studies the paradox of the situation of contemporary Indian women poets and the odyssey of their poetry from being a mere imitation of the great Romantic poets as it was initially to its strident search for identity and a more mundane acceptance of sexuality and the physical needs of women.

"Analysing Schizophrenic Experience in the Light of Psychoanalytical Feminism" explores a brief history of feminism and feminist theories, and Indian women's socio-literary background. Psychoanalytical theories have been discussed in detail and have been found very important in understanding the subjugation of women in patriarchy.

"Poetic Manifestations of Schizophrenic Experience" reveals the frustration, tension, bizarre behaviour, conflict, confusion, anxieties, depression, and contemplation of suicide as illustrated in the poetry of the poets taken for study.

"From Passivity to Stridency: Tackling the Experience" throws light on different methods employed by the poets to tackle the passivity imposed on them and the ensuing stridency in their tones and behaviour. The irony, ordinariness, confessional mode of Mamta Kalia, the love and sexuality in Gauri Deshpande, the allusive mode used by Suniti Namjoshi, the intense and highly personal poetry of Lalitha Venkateswaran, and the cryptic and bitter tone of Eunice de Souza have been investigated.

"Suniti Namjoshi's Poems: Striking a Different Note" examines Suniti Namjoshi's lesbian existence as a counter-attack on gender exploitation. Her bafflement as a diaspora has further complicated her situation.

The conflict between feminist leanings and tradition bound roles leading to schizophrenic experience and the ultimate reversion to resignation from a defiant stance of these poets need special consideration and finally after studying the similarities and differences in their poetry it has been concluded that this schizophrenic de-centring is a turning point in the growth of Indian English women poetry as the fecundity and experimentation of this poetry cannot be ignored.

I acknowledge the contribution of Dr. Rupinder Kaur, Professor, Dept of English, Punjabi University, Patiala for inspiring and guiding me throughout the project. I express my sincerest gratitude for making herself available whenever I needed.

I am deeply indebted to my parents, husband, sisters and my kids Smridh and Sarisha for their motivation and active cooperation.

Finally, I thank Prestige Books for bringing out the book so expeditiously and elegantly.

TANU GUPTA

Between Conformity and Rebellion: A Brief Survey of Contemporary Indian Women's Poetry

The "story" of Indian poetry began in 1830 with Kashiprasad Ghoshe, who called himself the "first Hindoo who has ventured to publish a volume of English poems" (Naik, *Echo* 27). It was Henry Derozio, however, who, with the publication of his poems in 1827, initiated the emergence of poetic creation in English by Indians. Most early efforts were made out of gratitude and emulation and are derivative and imitative in nature. There are, however, some honourable exceptions that deserve due credit and recognition. Indian English women's poetry took its origin in the process of Westernization in the later half of the nineteenth century and developed gradually into an essential aspect of the total Indian poetic consciousness as expressed in English. "It can safely be asserted that the 'Fair Voice' in Indian poetry in English is not a 'sparrow's voice,' it is a 'true voice of feeling'" (Chavan 121).

Toru Dutt (1856-1877) and Sarojini Naidu (1879-1949) were the first two great predecessors of contemporary Indian English women poets. Toru Dutt renders authenticity to the Indian English verse with her innovative style, representing extensively the Indian tradition in a foreign language. Her poetic contribution is eight original poems—"Miscellaneous" pieces in *Ancient Ballads and Legends*. The major subjects of her poetry are nature, love, home and all the poems reveal her narrative and descriptive skill. The Indian world of myths and legends is authentically portrayed for the first time in her ballads. Sometimes she can be seen anxious about women and their fate. In her well-known poem "Our Casuarina Tree," Toru Dutt writes:

> What is that dirge-like murmur that I hear
> Like the sea breaking on the shingle-beach?
> It is the tree's lament, an eerie speech,
> That haply to the unknown land may reach. (30-33)

Her unfinished novel called *Bianca or the Young Spanish Maiden* at some places "touches upon questions of gender, race and class without being very explicit" (Pathak 16).

Sarojini Naidu (1879-1940), popularly known as the "Nightingale of India," has been the most prominent woman poet of the colonial period who has won great acclaim in India and abroad. She was conscious of the woman's predicament which she has voiced in quite a few poems. Her poems reveal her "ambiguous attitude." Eunice de Souza points out: "Though she campaigned against 'purdah,' her poem 'Purdah' is imbued with nostalgia and exotic appeal: 'Her life is a revolving dream/ Of languid and sequestered ease'" (de Souza 3). She feels concerned for the desperate condition of widows, but, at the same time, in her maudlin voice, she seems to be endorsing the practice of "Sati." Even the poet's friend James Cousins disapproves of some of her poems because of their "perpetuation of the 'door-mat' attitude to womanhood . . . that masculine domination has sentimentalized into a virtue" (Cousins 261-62). Even Rabindranath Tagore who created "strong women" in his works like *Ghare-Baire* (1916), prescribed submissive behaviour for women in his prose writings:

> Woman has to be ready to suffer. She cannot allow her emotions to be dulled or polluted, for these are to create her life's atmosphere, apart from which her world would be dark and dead. (163)

The post-1947 era, that is the period after India gained independence, is marked by the country's search for her own identity as a new-born nation in the modern world. This search for identity is also reflected as one of the remarkable features of literature produced by contemporary Indian writers. P. Lal and K. Raghavendra Rao, in a somewhat brash "Introduction" of *Modern Indo-Anglian Poetry* (1958) declare that "the phase of Indo-Anglian romanticism ended with Sarojini Naidu." They emphasize "the need for the private voice," especially because "we live in an age that tends so easily to demonstrations of mass-approval and hysteria" (Qtd. Naik, *History* 193). The same is the case with the Indian English women poets of the post-independence period. They have little in common with the earlier generation of Indian women writing sentimental and romantic poetry in English in the nineteenth and early twentieth century. The poetry of these new poets is born out of their intense experience as women. They "have articulated as overtly and boldly as male poets" (K. Singh 47). Their poetry has now taken for its theme various Indian subjects from legend, folklore, to contemporary Indian situations: "The canvas became wide and interests more varied. Thus the real flowering of their genius came in the post-independence era" (Bajaj 16).

There is a remarkable shift in the poems of contemporary Indian women poets from eulogizing and spiritualizing love to a more mundane acceptance of sexuality and the physical needs of women. These poets have discovered their own voices and developed their sensibilities. Their poetry expresses the desire of woman to get away from the ties that have restricted her since time immemorial: "Some women poets, in particular, have made worthwhile attempts at mapping out new terrains as human beings and also as creative writers" (Pathak 15).

This contemporary poetry reveals the frustrations and tensions which women face because of the discrepancy between the way they want to behave and the way they are made to behave. The entrenched patriarchal structure still continues to control and restrict the lives of women in one way or the other. It still considers that women are someone's daughters, wives or mothers, minus their own personality. Before marriage they are brought up under strict control according to the traditional code with the view that they are to be given to the new master, their husband.

> Patriarchy, which is the ruling social system almost all over the world, ordains that woman's place is the home, her role as a wife and mother is quite often synonymous with her total human existence. (Dey 9)

The patriarchal practices are further perpetuated by myths and traditions which unfortunately have been embedded in the fabric of every society. According to V.A. Novarra, the myth related to the role of a woman in Britain prescribes that "a mother should devote herself to providing a secure environment for her children. A married woman cannot pursue her career which demands mobility" (Novarra 317).

In India, a woman is considered to be an embodiment of sacrifice and silent suffering. She should be virtuous, chaste, submissive, homely, graceful, and devoted to her husband and his family. She must seek pleasure in these relationships. Thus, the greatest crisis for a woman as Rukmini Nair explains is:

> A woman is a thing apart
> She is bracketed off, a
> Comma, semi-colon, at most
> A lower-case letter, lost. ("Margins, ma(i)nstream" 1-4)

The hint of any such ideas that one "exists primarily for the realization of oneself can never occur to her in the faintest of her dreams" (Jha 95). These attitudes exemplify the belief that woman should not have any right of her own; that she has only duties in relation to man. Kamala Das also articulates the plight and predicament of woman whom she considers doomed to live in an intensely man-made world:

> Dress in sarees, be girl
> Be wife, they said. Be embroiderer, be cook,
> Be a quarreller with servants. Fit in, Oh,
> Belong, cried the categorizers. ("An Introduction"45-48)

In a patriarchal society, the birth of a female child is traditionally less welcome than that of the male. Being born a boy is itself a privilege. Girls arrive in the world as undesirable creatures and the life-long battle against their formidable foe, i.e., their sex begins, as Eunice de Souza expresses in her "de Souza Prabhu" where she puts herself in the category of "lame ducks." In "One Man's Poetry" she says:

> As I grew up
> I longed only
> to laugh easily.
> All that emerged
> was a nervous whinny. (25-29)

As a daughter Mamta Kalia is haunted by the father figure. Father in her case becomes a symbol of male-dominance:

> Women like this relationship as this is the only male relationship which provides protection and affection without the physical in it. It is disliked as father is the first dominating male in life and a representative of the patriarchal society. (Bajaj 69)

In her poem "A Tribute to Papa" Mamta Kalia pays a different kind of tribute to her father, stating that her ideas and values clash with those of her father: "Everything about you clashes with nearly/ everything about me" (25-26). The mutual disillusionment has grown so much that she even thinks of "disowning" her father and his sacredness. Thus, the dichotomous attitude which continues to operate throughout a woman's life starts right in her parents' home.

The contemporary poets show no respect or gratitude for their mothers. The relationship does not seem to be very pleasant, close or satisfactory. Eunice de Souza in her "Forgive Me, Mother" confesses that "In dreams" (11), she "hacks" (12) her mother.

According to Hodding Carter Jr., "there are two lasting bequests we should give our children . . . one is roots, the other is wings" (Qtd. M. Gupta 44). However, parents encourage the development of roots in girls and simultaneously minimize the importance of wings. They discriminate against the girls, right from their birth. As a result, the relationship cannot become a satisfying one. Sunita Jain, great in her anguish, tries to be good towards her mother:

> I have tried not to curse you. ("Mother" 9)

In a traditional social set-up when young girls reach puberty, their movements are restricted whereas there are no restrictions for their brothers who are of the same age group. The double standards start operating from this age, binding girls indoors and encouraging boys to develop outdoor activities. A spirit of competition, exploration and challenge is inculcated among boys, and they are taught to exert their supremacy over the world in general. Girls, on the contrary, are discouraged from showing aggressive behaviour and, instead, feminine virtues of grace, modesty and self-effacement are frequently demanded from them as Sunita Jain says in an interview:

> My brother who was two years older to me used to feel jealous of me because of my better academic record. He used to pull my 'choti,' push me down, fight with me and when I used to curse him I was told not to do the same as he was my brother. (Jain)

The same crisis has been faced by many women poets. Monika Varma has felt this pressure:

> I climbed tree. . . .
> get down at once
> It is most unsuitable for young ladies,
> the governess, Louisa M. Bayley said ("Disremember Me Doves")

The dichotomous attitude thus begins early in life and lasts throughout a woman's existence. She is continuously reminded of her femininity. Lakshmi Kannan was instructed:

> No. Don't run
> don't take long strides
> don't raise voice
> be a woman, be moderate in everything. ("An Omen")

Sujatha Modayil says that she was happy at twelve that she had become a woman but as she grew up she realized the male dominance and superiority:

> Hold your breath now, girls,
> The game is nearly over
> The power and glory, our's
> For ever and ever. ("The Little Madams")

This secondary status becomes more obvious as a girl grows up. She is prevented from developing her own individuality. She is constantly reminded that she is destined for man and the one who gets the most masculine attention is the luckiest one. Entire rearing and gearing up of a girl is male-oriented and her salvation lies in marriage. Parents, grandparents, uncles, aunts—all condition her for this destiny right from her childhood. Sujata Bhatt in her poem "Light" expresses this tragic fate of being a daughter:

> When I was seventeen
> My grandmother said
>   'Get her married
>   before the light
>   goes out of her face.'

Sunita Jain's mother also forced her into marriage. At "the tender age of 18," she became someone's "bhabhi," "chachi," and "mami." Thus, a woman in the male dominated society is conditioned into the emotional and cognitive traits of subordination and dependence. She is looked down upon as a transitory member of the family in contrast with her brothers, who are supposed to be the transmitters of the family name to future generations and are, therefore, more carefully and lovingly brought up and given more advantages.

Ironically, these girls believe that marriage is an escape from the control of parents and society. Imtiaz Dharker's Fatimah, a Muslim girl, elopes with an English boy to free herself from the shackles of the closed Muslim world but it turns out to be only an exchange of masters:

> And there you are with your English boy
> Who was going to set you free,
> Trying to smile and be accepted,
> Always on your knees. ("Purdah and Other Poems")

Thus, marriage for a girl means only an exchange of masters—first it is the parents who control, now there will be husband. As Simone de Beauvoir observes:

> There is unanimous agreement that getting a husband—or in some cases a 'protector'—is for her the most important of undertakings. . . . She will free herself from the parental home, from her mother's hold, she will open up her future, not by active conquest but by delivering herself up, passive and docile, into the hands of a new master. (352)

Marriage does not turn out to be a companionship or equality for a woman; rather it is a trap which negates her rights to individuality, independence and self-realization. It thwarts the growth of individuality in Lalitha Venkateswaran. At seventeen she was dreaming about self-growth and her adolescent ambitions were:

> All learning would be stormed by me.
> I would sing, make speeches, read the news;
> Write, act, run offices and marathons.
> I would concentrate upon myself. ("Building" 9-12)

But then entered the man and the damage was irreparable:

> You
> Did not belong in my plans; and so
> My house broke up to keep you whole.
> The construction costs were terrible. (*Ibid.* 15-18)

She found herself echoing "your punch-lines, your actions, your exits" (11) in "Debit." Relationship with man has entailed the loss of identity for Sunita Jain also:

> To grow to your size

I chopped my wings;
our creature existence
I thought would be
bliss. ("When You Fell, My Love" 1-5)

It is a frustrating experience as she sets up house for her husband and realizes even the children were "his children." She is subjugated and sidelined and usually her position is no better than the poor, oppressed and racial minorities like the blacks. The "power politics" (25) to use a phrase from Kate Millett, operates in a subtle manner in the institution of marriage, reducing the status of a woman to a mere utility item, an object for decoration, for possession and for man's sexual gratification.

In her book *Women, Resistance and Revolution*, Sheila Rowbotham uses the term "colonialized" to show the oppressed status of women in the society. She cites "economic dependence," "cultural takeover" and "the identification of dignity with resemblance to the oppressor" as some of "the similarities that exist between the colonization of the underdeveloped countries and female oppression" (2014). J.S. Mill is right in saying that marriage is the worst form of slavery for women. He says: "No slave is a slave to the same lengths, and in so full a sense of words, as a wife is" (Mill 124). Engels in his *The Origin of the Family* also points out that the Latin word *Familia* means the total number of slaves belonging to one man. In marriage a man enjoys both the worlds: of home and of career. Marriage to him means enlargement and confirmation of his existence. It permits him progression and self-advancement. A woman on the other hand is virtually reduced to the status of a maid. Mamta Kalia complains of the effect of being a housewife on her individuality and seems to be frustrated and dissatisfied:

I, no longer feel I'm Mamta Kalia
I am Kamla
Or Vimla
Or Kanta or Shanta. ("Anonymous" 1-4)

The pressure of kitchen-work and household work becomes a threat to a woman's freedom and individuality. This traditional drudgery of household chores is depressing:

> Unmade beds, dirty linen
> Papers wrongfolded, slippers thrown,
> Bulging ashtrays,
> Lidless tubes of toothpastes, hair cream,
> Unwashed brushes,
> Buttonless shirts, laceless shoes,
> A sinkful of plates,
> And a head full of ache.
> ("Love Made a Housewife Out of Me" 12-19)

Sunita Jain also shows the same signs of discontentment with the domestic duties. The everyday household concerns such as "years of washing dishes" and the like give her a "creasing forehead." "She wanted marriage to be a relationship of mutual understanding and sharing, but it turned out to be a fool's paradise" (K. Singh 73). In her poem "Knife" she expresses the destructive influence of household drudgery:

> My chapped feet,
> my hands grown rough with domestic duties,
> where shall I hide these.

Years of household chores give women parched, blistered and scratched hands. To Sujata Bhatt:

> now her fist
> looks more like her heart
> open wounds ("Red August")

Many relationships are imposed on a woman in marriage. As a result she has to be subservient not only to her husband but also to all those who belong to her husband. Behroze Shroff has exposed this reality of Indian marriage, wifehood and motherhood in her poem "Mother." She shows how a girl's cherished dreams are destroyed at the tender age of nineteen:

> Your youth and energy were harnessed

To serve a mother-in-law's sick bed.

Joint family is a great crusher of a woman's happiness. Mamta Kalia also feels the disparaging influence of this system as she says:

> I wanted to tell them how I wept in bed all night once
> And struggle hard from hurting myself.
> That it wasn't easy to be happy in a family of twelve.
> ("After Eight Years of My Marriage" 15-17)

She takes her husband's name, his religion, family and class. Before marriage she is moulded by her parents and afterwards "a wife is what her husband makes her" (Beauvoir 484). In her "Matrimonial Bliss," she is all "disjointed" inside and feels that she keeps hanging on her husband like an "appendix." Taking stock of her life during his absence, she realizes:

> In reality
> all our friends were your friends,
> all our ideas your ideas
> all our projects your projects.
> I followed you like a corollary. ("Sunday Song" 40-44)

Nothing belongs to her and she belongs nowhere. Ironically enough, her only possessions are amenorrhea and gas-trouble which she doesn't want to disclose to her husband:

> I've started yawning too much,
> And watching my nails not grow.
> I've also developed gas trouble and amenorrhoea,
> But I don't want to tell you
> Or you'll send for a doctor
> And rob me even of these. ("Matrimonial Bliss" 28-33)

She eventually finds, as Germaine Greer observes, that after marriage her life has "changed radically but not her husband's" (321).

Throughout history, women have been appropriated as sexual objects. Karl Marx says, "*Marriage* . . . is incontestably a form of *exclusive private property*" (Qtd. Mitchell 110) and this is echoed by Gauri Deshpande who expresses about this position of a woman in marriage in her poem "Man and Woman":

> That she could with such ease
> be enslaved by your skilful hands
> beggar's heart and from himalayan heights
> condescend to warm your bed
> stiffen your manhood
> and bear your spawn. (Qtd. Barbuddhe 267)

She reveals how a woman, torn ruthlessly between fulfillment and frustration, is forced to accept her identity as a lonely being:

> When from the good fortune
> of smiles and caresses
> we move into the inexplicable
> unintelligible darkness
> of sorrow, delay, departure, suspicion ("The Eclipse" 1-5)

Mamta Kalia's "I am a Great Fool" also presents the poet's sense of ennui in her matrimonial relationship, where she finds marriage as hazardous to keeping love alive. She cries in disillusionment:

> I am a great fool
> To think that marriage is bliss,
> Was it last month or last year
> That we exchanged a kiss. (1-4)

Margaret Chatterjee reveals the same painful experience of a woman when a man leaves after having gratified his sexual appetite:

> Loving quickly he
> Turned his back,
> while soundlessly
> She wept
> Into the night. ("Scars")

Talking about this sense of loneliness which exists in marital relationships, Greer says: "many a housewife staring at the back of their husband's newspaper, or listening to his breathing in bed is lonelier than any spinster in a rented room" (Greer 244). Most of the women suffer in marriage because their husbands like to remain locked up in their solitary cells and do not try to recognize the fact that love is necessary to happiness.

Extra-marital relations are no solutions to the marital problems. The commission of adultery in case of Kamala Das could not fulfil her quest for an ideal lover.

> After that love became a swivel-door
> When one went out, another came in.
> Then I lost count, for always in my arms
> Was a substitute for a substitute. ("Substitute" 9-12)

It is only love, candour, consent, companionship and tenderness within marriage that a woman longs for. Otherwise, marriage turns out to be an unpleasant experience.

Contemporary Indian women poets realized that real self or natural self is totally denied to a married woman and who knows it better than Kamala Das. A woman in marriage has to play imposed roles:

> I must pose
> I must pretend,
> I must act the role
> of a happy woman,
> Happy wife. ("The Suicide" 41-45)

A double life is the fate of a married woman. As her husband arrives, Mamta Kalia pretends to be happy:

> I put all of me together
> And give you my best smile
> That's eternally saying cheese. ("Matrimonial Bliss" 19-21)

Love for a man is a temporary refuge from boredom and loneliness. For a woman love means complete emotional involvement. She wants a lasting and stable relationship with man. Man looks upon sex as a means of self-gratification and sensual pleasure whereas woman relates it to the emotional fulfillment and meaning in life. Sex seems to a woman a mere dry activity that leaves her unsatisfied. Gauri Deshpande expresses that men do not penetrate into the "plunging depths" of women's "souls/and bodies" ("No More" 3-4). In her "Re: Memories" there is much anguish and tears:

> A stillness before sleep
> And an awareness in dreams.
> You should be left with a face at the window
> A heartbreak, a farewell.
> Otherwise there's nothing. (10-14)

Gauri Deshpande is, thus, primarily concerned with the exploration of the various intricacies and conflicts of the man-woman relationship. She depicts woman as distressed by the non-fulfillment of physical as well as emotional cravings. Kanwar Dinesh Singh while discussing her poetry expresses:

> She finds the lack of genial 'afterplay' in lovemaking as most unsatisfying and disappointing. In the whole gamut of lovemaking she perceives neither physical intensity nor mental satisfaction, and finds neither emotional contentment nor even spiritual delight. (76)

The lack of emotional content in man-woman relationship has been the cause of frustration in Kamala Das also. Lovemaking to Kamala Das is, as Anisur Rahman puts it, "a painful union with only a remote hope of discovering something meaningful" (49). Kamala Das describes her experiences in "Convicts":

> That was the only kind of love,
> This hacking at each other's parts
> Like convicts hacking, breaking clods
> At noon. (*The Descendents* 26)

Sunita Jain also finds this experience disgusting as men often treat women as objects of lust:

> —take me
> still, not as a lover
> in love's renewed mystery
> but in lust parasitic. (*Sensum* 130)

She seeks communion along with the corporeal, at the levels of mind and heart. She wants her lover to "Come closer . . ./ closer in mind" (*Ibid* 116) She asserts:

> Slowly. My love,
> use words
> till touch
> is feeling. (*Ibid.* 130)

She "brings forth the altered attitude of the modern woman who is not just a corpus of flesh and blood, but she does have a heart and mind also" (K. Singh 68):

> I want you to say
> You love me
> As leaves grow
> On clinging vines—. . .
> till music, hard and clean
> like river water on stones,
> courses through my soul-chime. (*Ibid* 112)

There is a lack of romantic idealism in the experience of love. Almost all the poems from Mamta Kalia's second vol. *Poems '78* project the tension of surviving through the boredom of marriage. The poet in her deep sadness explores her relationship with her husband:

> You glare when I come
> And growl when I talk
> And sulk when I'm mum,
> And frown when I laugh.
> You nag when I near
> And swear when I cheer
>
> ("Love Made a Housewife Out of Me" 45-50)

She further says:

> You get mad if I read
> You get mad if I don't.
> You get mad if I teach Anu,
> You get mad if I won't. (*Ibid* 53-56)

Suniti Namjoshi's poetry, too, shows her disillusionment with love. She seems to be so much disgusted with the physical in love that she talks always of sex in a satirical tone. In her "Benefits" she says, "Together we'll make/ many bastards" (8-9). While reading her, Dwivedi says, she "seems to be engulfed with a deep sense of horror and disgust in the matter of love and sex" (208).

Moreover, a woman is considered to be an instrument for continuing her husband's family. The pressure of maternity for a son's birth is usually faced by a woman. Behroze Shroff expresses that even at the risk of a woman's life her "production unit" is made to function time and again till a son is born:

> Like a bucket of water
> Scraped out of low-lying well,
> a son was obtained from you. ("In Their Own Voice")

If a woman gives birth to a male child, she is considered to be lucky. In her poem "Bridge and the Tea Party" Behroze Shroff has beautifully captured this fact through a dialogue of four mothers. She shows how it is Bunty's mother who holds the trump card and emerges as the victor:

> I'll call Bunty
> darling sing what
> teacher taught you
> sing near aunty.

Even after giving birth to a son, a woman is relegated to the background. The birth is considered to be a "product" of the "holy efforts" of each aunt and uncle. Instead of the mother, the father is congratulated:

> The father made hero
> was congratulated, praised, feted
> The mother was given
> tips on child-bearing. ("In Their Own Voice")

The children also show no gratitude to their mothers when they grow up. Gauri Deshpande in her "The Female of the Species" talks of this "ungratefulness of children" (3) as a common feature. This filial relationship adds to the crisis of a woman. Sunita Jain in her poems expresses, how her visits to her daughter's rooms are frowned upon as intrusion upon privacy. She says:

> Is blood red even now?
> Are prayers made?
> Does joy still light up
> a child's face?
> One by one I lay to rest
> what in you was mine. ("Daughter 2" 9-14)

Mamta Kalia also presents a very realistic view:

> No,
> I am no pelican to my sons
> Nor a dove to my love.
> I am an antibiotic against all infections.
> ("No, I am no Pelican to my Sons" 2-5)

Further, in her poem "I Must Write Nicely Now" she says, "You can't adjust with your own children" as they come to have their own individuality.

Even the economically independent woman's lot is no better. She has to bear the double burden—of job and household responsibilities. At home her contribution is seldom recognized while at working place she is treated as inferior or is harassed or exploited. She finds it hard to cope with the tedium of daily routine. She feels sandwiched between her place of work and household. Mamta Kalia expresses this fate of a working woman as on one hand, she has to bear the drudgery of her workplace, and on the other she has to manage "sinkful of plates." In her poem "How like a Fool" she tells about her exhaustion and humiliation in the office:

> Here like a fool I've been working all along
> When work is work's own defeat.
> My promotion waits on your naughty knees
> Readiness is all I now need. (1-4)

Her boss takes her to task for being late and then as his eyes make dent right down her shoulders, his mood changes. The poet understands all this but refuses to oblige:

> He stared till he could stare no longer.
> And his eyes made dents right down my shoulders.
> I suddenly knew he was angry no longer,
> But I wasn't in a mood to be his hamburger
> So I asked for a charge sheet
> And came out. ("Either You are Born with It" 11-16)

She wants to "even up" everything with her boss and wants to "hit" him with "a stone" (24) as she herself has tasted "the whole death" (7) for "twenty-three years" (9):

> You made me kneel
> for insignificant things;
> you made me feel
> the wrong thing relevant
> No, more than that,
> you made a cipher out of me
> that you could add or subtract easily. ("Tit for Tat"10-16)

She also expresses the same sentiment in her poem "An Active Life." The poem brings forth the dreary routine of a female lecturer whose daily schedule includes preparing for "lectures" and "jotting down dictionary meanings" (8), and on Sundays, she engages herself in watching movie or writing diary or reading some book borrowed from the library. And by the end of the day:

> She gargled at night
> and sleep serenely
> after a bit of mental masturbation. (18-20)

However, problems arise when a woman too starts seeking direction for herself. No longer content with what life doles out, she wants to set her own agenda.

> It appears perfectly natural that Indian women elevate their voice against the established order and try to affirm their distinct identity

> by breaking the traditional taboos as to love and sex which is the outcome of male-dominated society. (R. Gupta 45)

The same is the case with the contemporary Indian women's poetry. It has tried to break the boundaries of tradition. Kamala Das is regarded as a champion of freedom for women. She introduces a new trend in Indian poetry in English with her bold, ruthless honesty tearing passionately at conventional attitudes to reveal the quintessential woman within.

Kamala Das has modernized the Indian feminine poetic psyche. Her poetry expresses a woman's longing for independence and freedom, quest for an individual identity, hunger for establishing a meaningful relationship with a man, with the outside world. She emerges as a staunch rebel against the customary patriarchal arrangement in the Indian society, expressing "her inability to conform to the behavioural pattern expected in a tradition ridden family" (Pathak 19). The persona in her poems breaks away from the traditional role of a woman:

> Then . . . I wore a shirt and my
> Brother's trousers, cut my hair short and ignored
> My womanliness. ("An Introduction" 33-35)

She suffers badly from the identity crisis. She is displeased with the kind of social conditioning and gender stereotyping a woman is subjected to right from her childhood days. She persistently protests against this "soul killing" subjugation and planning "to tame a swallow" and asks: "Woman, is this happiness, this lying buried \ Beneath a man?" ("The Conflagration"). Her poems are a powerful expression of her feminine sensibility which seeks self-realization through man's love. She revolts against conventions, and struggles to realize her desire for ideal love through extra-marital sexual relationships. The urge for freedom from living with the husband makes her rebellious:

> I shall some day leave, leave the cocoon
> You built around me with morning tea. ("Summer in Calcutta" 52)

Mamta Kalia also rebels against patriarchy and the inhibiting world of middle-class respectability. Such poems are haunted by the memories of her father:

> But you've always wanted to be a model man,
> A sort of an ideal.
> When you can't think of doing anything,
> You start praying,
> Spending useless hours at the temple. ("Tribute to Papa" 12-16)

A desire for living naturally can also be seen in her poetry:

> I was elated to find
> you couldn't stand *The Faery Queen,*
> *dahi vadas* and arranged marriages.
> And you were delighted to see me
> in an ill-fitting kurta,
> a fag and minus-four glasses. ("Made for Each Other" 5-10)

The young women of today reflect an awareness of the biased attitude of the society. They have started asserting their individuality by challenging the taboos and destructive social norms. "Debit" expresses Lalitha Venkateswaran's unresolved tension:

> I catch myself echoing
> Your punch-lines, your actions, your exits.
> I would escape your circle if I could do. (10-12)

Sunita Jain in her "They Prey" also feels like a "prey" engaged in an unequal fight against the "anglers." And in her "It's a Promise" she tries to go against all this orthodoxy and wants to assert herself:

> I shall (it's a promise)
> Sing once again
> of all that you
> my darling
> killed. (*Sensum* 143)

The poetry of these poets expresses a woman's longing for independence and freedom, quest for an individual identity, hunger for establishing a meaningful relationship with a man, with the outside world. Monika Varma's "Give me Space" shows her feelings of repression perhaps under the pressure of patriarchy. She demands for a space "for one little day" before she dies:

> Give me space . . .
> space not just to exist
> but live . . .

The freedom loving feminine selves of these women poets often result in an ego clash with their husbands. And it becomes difficult for both of them to arrive at a consensus as it is in the case of Mamta Kalia:

> Every time I open my mouth,
> You feel let down,
> And every time you discuss your pay scale,
> I try hard not to frown.
> If this goes on where will we end?
> Or have we ended before we have begun?
>
> ("Dubious Lovers" 16-21)

Contemporary Indian English women poetry appears to be seriously involved with the power struggle to dislodge patriarchy. "It is more realistic, direct, intense and explorative than men" (Chavan 113). These poets question the very foundations of patriarchal assumptions. There has been an increasing tendency among them to redefine their own selves. Vijaya Goel tries to jolt women out of their complacency:

> You are the power of this earth,
> The creator of man,
> Yet you lie at his feet,
> Begging to survive! ("She")

However, in forging new identities, new metaphors and symbols, new bonds and new meanings, these poets experience a conflict between their personal values and larger social practices. The weight of an entire cultural tradition that has relegated and marginalized them is too great to be either borne or cast off. The traditional make-up of conventional women is a factor which persistently forbids them from breaking away completely from the role of traditional wife. Thus, their attitude becomes double edged: rebellious and tender. Their struggle with themselves and the world outside for a kind of refuge in the realm of freedom takes the form of a conflict between passivity and rebellion against the male-oriented universe. The poetry of contemporary Indian English women poets speaks for and interprets these truths of their gender.

> It operates within two divergent pulls—an impulse towards a genuinely independent definition of the self on the one hand and the stronghold of patriarchal social reality tending towards their self-effacement on the other. (Beniwal 72)

Torn between their feminist desires on one side and the stereotyped social roles on the other, the poems of these poets are constructed differently as compared to the poems of the male writers.

Mamta Kalia in her conversation with Eunice de Souza in the latter's book *Talking Poems: Conversations with Poets* concedes that even if you "equip yourself academically, professionally; you cannot hope others will move at the same pace." And this, she reiterates, "brings about a crisis in your attitude" (61). "With characteristic nonchalance, Kalia admits that she too is caught up like others before her, in the ubiquitous double bind of the woman writer" (M. Singh 168). Straddling the two worlds of tradition and modernity, freedom and bondage, domesticity and professionalism, her creative graph has been wavering between "flashes and crashes." This vacillation between two extremes results in her divided consciousness.

Gauri Deshpande also strongly feels that a woman has to compromise and adapt to the circumstances she is situated in. But at the same time in such circumstances she can neither have tranquillity, nor peace of mind. A frustration results from the shock and despair she experiences in her life. She develops the "habit of pain" (8) and the grit of surviving in a milieu that is "meaningless" (7):

I just glimpsed the face in passing
Only mildly familiar, not really known
And wondered at the sudden gust of pain.
After an hour or two it came back again:
It was a face very like your own
—Your son or daughter, I'm certain— ("Souvenir" 1-6)

In her fiercely honest search for identity, Suniti Namjoshi reveals her inner contrasts, conflicts, emotions, feelings, ironies and extremes. Her poems move rapidly through sentiments, anger, sympathy and tensions. Her passionate quest for love in "Courtship" and her disillusionment in love in "When Butterflies Die" make her behaviour strange:

I recall your lies,
Some of your words,
And small gentlenesses.
When butterflies die, they do not smell.
The butterflies were lovely, weren't they? (3-7)

In Lalitha Venkateswaran's poem "Chitrangada" there is the agony of the deeply felt shock when the lover enters in her life:

Then you came to my door my love,
Disguised as a mendicant,
And took me unawares. (15-17)

And she finds her "spring" "full of tears" (19). The poem probes the agonizing experience of disappointment in love. Her poetry reveals her rage, grief, inner fears and her sense of betrayal. A sense of panic and insecurity is there:

No moon tonight. The dark
Snakes into corners.
Panic is a maddened horse
Bound in my shrinking heart. ("Attendance" 1-4)

So deeply ingrained is the feeling of being alienated and unwanted, in the poetry of these poets that they even attempt suicide as Eunice de Souza confesses in her "Autobiographical."

Although contemporary women poets are expressive about the freedom they claim for themselves as women, yet we can still find them having a suffocated existence. The lives of these women still revolve around the pivot of marriage. A heavy pressure is exerted by the society on them to pull on their marriage even if it is disintegrating. Male chauvinism has been taken for granted through the entire course of human evolution. If women have ever raised the question of the position of men in the society, the theme of sacrifice is dinned into their supple minds resulting in their divided selves.

The paradox of a woman's situation is that she is still expected to perform the roles both inside and outside the home with the same amount of devotion and fervour. She is also expected to maintain the demeanour, stay calm and remain placid whatever the circumstances may be. She feels equal to man and can compete with him in every sphere and yet she is still expected to follow the decorum of walking a step behind him wherever she goes. The desire to flout the rules, break traditions and the yearning for self-assertion are common themes in the poetry of Indian women. Their poems reflect the chasm that exists between their desires to do the things that have been hitherto denied them and the forced submission to what society allows them to do. They feel capable of doing much more than they are allowed to because the world which they inhabit exercises constraints, which in turn leads to frustration and discontentment. This is generally the woman's predicament; she feels the need to do greater things and yet realizes that the environment is uncongenial to her active participation in life. The contemporary Indian women poets are also sharing the same ambience and the same concerns of an average woman.

In the mind of a woman, there is always a conflict between her viriloid tendencies and feminine tendencies:

> Evidently to play at being a man will be for her a source of frustration; but to play at being a woman is also a delusion; to be a woman would mean to be the Object, the Other and the Other nev-

> ertheless remains subject in the midst of her resignation. (Beauvoir 83)

And this frustration results in her tending towards a schizophrenic existence as Anup Beniwal in his article "Identity, Experience, Aesthetics: Indian Women's Poetry in English" has aptly remarked about the poetry of Suniti Namjoshi: "the women in Suniti Namjoshi in their tentative exploration towards the direction of self-definition find themselves on the verge of schizophrenic existence." (78) And the same can be said about the other contemporary Indian women poets. From Kamala Das till now, women who are torn between their desires and a sense of loss, appear schizophrenic.

Schizophrenia, a serious brain disease, a state of mental impairment, results in frustration and depression. A person loses all interest and pleasure in life. He may feel frightened, anxious, confused or withdrawn. His bizarre behaviour takes him away from active social life. His delusions and hallucinations sometimes lead him to committing suicide. Sujatha Modayil during her stay in America during the summer of 1969 worked with chronic schizophrenics. In exploring the phenomenon of this mental disorder, she exposes the bitter truth of the human being's failure to live naturally:

> You who rebelled
> Against mindless wealth.
> You who realized that
> Life without the personal touch
> Is not life at all. ("We are Reconciled")

And this is perhaps descriptive of the dilemma of the women poets as well.

The aim of the present study is to explore this tendency as reflected in the selected works of some contemporary Indian English women poets, such as Mamta Kalia, Gauri Deshpande, Suniti Namjoshi, Lalitha Venkateswaran, Eunice de Souza, Sunita Jain and Debjani Chatterjee. The unusual tearfulness, depression, suicidal attempts, delusions, hallucinations, strange thinking and bizarre behaviour of these poets can be compared with those who lead a schizophrenic existence. All this doesn't mean that these poets are neurotic as they are not schizophrenic in the technical sense of the term; their condition is similar in many respects. Freud tells us that an "artist is not like a neurotic in that he knows how to find a way back from the world of imagination and once more get a firm foothold in reality" (Trilling 45). Anup Beniwal while discussing the tensions in the poetic sensibility of contemporary poets expresses:

> The Indian women's poetry, thus operates within two divergent pulls—an impulse towards a genuinely independent definition of the self on the one hand and the strong hold of patriarchal social reality tending towards their self-effacement on the other. This dichotomy invariably brings about tension in their poetic sensibility. (72)

But this tendency of charting out a "new woman" who questions and protests rather than lives in ignominy leads her to tread on problematic grounds, resulting in her divided existence.

Traditional expectations of the family, obligations to society, snatching away of the individual freedom, exploitation and hypocrisy and sham perpetuated in the name of matrimony . . . only resulted in the identity crisis. (Pathak 24)

And the hungry self of post-independence Indian women poets in their search for trust, companionship, security, love and dignity, confronts a variety of anomalies, contradictions and paradoxes. Contemporary women poets "are not all of a piece, any more than the males of the species are" (Iyengar 727). They find themselves caught between the conflict of tradition-bound self and the self looking for freedom and independence. The dualities within them leave them sad, lonely and empty. Vacillating between conformity and rebellion they get frustrated and disappointed, and hence, seem schizophrenic.

Works Cited

Bajaj, Rashmi. *Women Indo-Anglian Poets: A Critique*. New Delhi: Asian, 1996.

Barbuddhe, Satish. *Indian Literature in English: Critical Views*. New Delhi: Sarup, 2007.

Beauvoir, Simone de. *The Second Sex*. Trans. H.M. Parshley. New York: Vintage, 1952.

Beniwal, Anup. "Identity, Experience, Aesthetic: Indian Women's Poetry in English." *Occasional Papers* (March 1999): 71-95.

Chavan, Sunanda P. *The Fair Voice: The Study of Indian Women Poets in English*. New Delhi: Sterling, 1984.

Cousins, James H. *The Renaissance in India*. Madras: Ganesh, 1918.

Das, Kamala. *The Descendents*. Calcutta: Writers Workshop, 1973.

______. *The Old Playhouse and Other Poems*. 22 Feb. 2008 <http://books.google.co.in/books?id=eI8yp7jvmqAC&dq=kamala+das+the+old+playhouse&printsec=frontcover&source=in&hl=en&ei=JRuJS6W2GovCrAfz0JmfCg&sa=X&oi=book_result&ct=result&resnum=12&ved=0CC0Q6AEwCw#v=onepage&q=&f=fals

de Souza, Eunice, ed. *Nine Indian Women Poets: An Anthology*. New Delhi: Oxford, 1997.

Dey, Esha. "Woman as Object: The Feminine Condition in a Decadent Patriarchy." *The Literary Criterion* 10.4 (1985): 9-20.

Dutt, Toru. "Our Casuarina-Tree." *Representative Poetry Online*. 2009. University of Toronto Libraries. 2 Jan. 2010 <http:// rpo.library.utoronto.ca/poem/2685.html>.

Dwivedi, A.N., ed. *Papers on Indian Writing in English*. 2nd ed. Vol. 1. New Delhi: Atlantic, 2001.

Greer, Germaine. *The Female Eunuch*. St. Albana: Paladin, 1976.

Gupta, Meenakshi. "The Girl Child: A Psychological Perspective." *The Girl Child in Twentieth Century Indian Literature*. Ed. Vinay Kirpal. Delhi: Sterling, 1992. 44-52.

Gupta, Ramesh Kumar. "A Feminist Voice—A Study of Kamala Das's Poems." *Indian English Literature*. Ed. Basavaraj Naikar. Vol. 3. New Delhi: Atlantic, 2002. 39-45.

India-Poetry International Web. 23 Mar. 2007 < http:// india.poetry internationalweb.org/piw_cms/cms/cms_module/index.php?obj_id=2736&x=1>.

Iyengar, K.R. Srinivasa. *Indian Writing in English*. 5th ed. Delhi: Sterling, 1985.

Jain, Sunita. *Sensum: Collected Poems (1965-2000)*. New Delhi: Read Books, 2007.

_____. Personal Interview. 30 June 2007.

Jha, Akhilesh. *Modernization and the Hindu Socio-Culture*. Delhi: B.R., 1978.

Kalia, Mamta. Interview with Eunice de Souza. *Talking Poems: Conversations with Poets*. New Delhi: Oxford UP, 1999. 57-66.

King, Bruce. *Modern Indian Poetry in English*. Delhi: Oxford UP, 1987.

Mill, J.S. *The Subjection of Women*. 4th ed. London: Longmans, 1878.

Millett, Kate. *Sexual Politics*. New York: Doubleday, 1970.

Mitchell, Juliet. *Woman's Estate*. New York: Vintage, 1973.

Mitra, Amitabh. "End of a Rite: Kamala Das Passes Away." 31 May 2009. *Discritics.org*. 31 June 2009 <http://desicritics.org/ 2009/05/ 31/123741.php>.

Naik, M.K. *A History of Indian English Literature*. Delhi: Sahitya Akademi, 1982.

_____. "Echo and Voice in Indian Poetry in English." *Contemporary Indian English Verse: An Evaluation*. Ed. Chirantan Kulshrestha. New Delhi: Arnold-Heinemann, 1980. 26-40.

Novarra, V.A. "International Women's Year 1975." *Contemporary Review*. 1313 (June1975).

Pathak, R.S. "Indian Women Poets: Mapping out New Terrains." *Journal of Indian Writing in English*. 29 (July 2001): 14-26.

Rahman, Anisur. *Expressive Form in the Poetry of Kamala Das*. New Delhi: Abhinav, 1981.

Rowbotham, Sheila. *Women, Resistance, and Revolution*. New York: Pantheon, 1972.

Singh, Kanwar Dinesh. *Feminism and Postfeminism: The Context of Modern Indian Women Poets Writing in English*. New Delhi: Sarup, 2004.

Singh, Mina Surjit. *Six Women Poets: A Cross-Cultural Study*. New Delhi: Prestige, 2003.

Tagore, Rabindranath. *Creative Unity*. London: Macmillan, 1922.

Trilling, Lionel. *The Liberal Imagination: Essays on Literature and Society*. New York: Viking Press, 1950.

Schizophrenic Experience in the Light of Psychoanalytical Feminism

> Women of every race are the only discriminated group with no territory, no country of their own, not even a neighbourhood. In a patriarchy a poor man's house may be his castle but even a rich woman's body is not her own. Somewhere in our lives each of us needs a free place, a little psychic territory. (Steinem)

Feminism is the consequence of the culture or society shaped and governed by men to suit their own interests regardless of women's basic needs and happiness. During the 1990s, feminism has lost the fervour and enthusiasm it enjoyed in 1960s and 1970s as it is believed that its relevance has declined now that woman has succeeded in striding shoulder to shoulder with man in all walks of life. Feminism as a movement earned a backlash. The backlash has taken different forms at different times in history, but some characteristic patterns seem to emerge repeatedly. These include stereotyping feminists and their ideas as crazy, outrageous, or trivial; insisting on immutable differences created by God or Nature that make social change impossible; and characterizing feminism as a mere quarrel among women. The media, too, started declaring feminism as outdated:

> claiming that equal rights have been fully achieved, society is now in a 'postfeminist' era, and women are abandoning feminism because it has proved to have terrible consequences. In the 1980s version of backlash, everything from infertility to the breakdown of society was blamed on feminism. (Crawford 10)

In a recent essay, "The War against Feminism," Nancy Gibbs states:

> Throughout history, any time women tried to loosen their corsets and breathe more freely, they met with a suffocating counterattack. . . . First the fundamental right, then the White House and ultimately Hollywood, television and many journalists held feminism responsible for every woe besetting women, from mental depression to meager savings accounts, from teenage suicides to eating disorders to bad complexions. The collective message to women went like this: Feminism is your worst enemy. (Gibbs 43)

As a result most women stopped appreciating and applauding feminism though they felt the need for a strong women's movement.

Despite attempts to discredit the goals of feminism, the majority of women still endorse many of the goals. They have a supportive opinion of feminism and the women's movement. They "describe feminism as strong, caring, open-minded, knowledgeable and intelligent" (Crawford 11). However, they are very reluctant to label themselves feminists, demonstrating that simply adding the "f-word" (feminist) causes people to think more negatively about a group.

Moreover, the situation differs from country to country as the feminists of the Third World countries are asserting nowadays. Thus, "the feminist movement is going quite strong; with the prospects of getting stronger in the near future . . . it is unmistakably spreading in most of the countries of Third World like wildfire" (Sharma 189). Hence, the need is to ponder over it and discuss it to make it really meaningful.

Feminism, as a movement, began late in the 18th century more particularly with Mary Wollstonecraft's *A Vindication of the Rights of Women* (1792) which is regarded as the manifesto of modern feminism. She demanded equal opportunity for a woman in the field of education, economics and politics. Later came John Stuart Mill's *The Subjection of Women* (1869). He felt that economic independence is essential for the dignity of woman. Virginia Woolf's *A Room of One's Own* (1929) is classic document of the feminist critical movement. How woman looks at herself as a human being with her own distinctive sensibility is emphasized herein. Dorothy Richardson's 12 vol. stream-of-consciousness novel *Pilgrimage* also centres on the female consciousness of the heroine, Miriam Henderson.

An important landmark in the evolution of the feminist criticism in the post-war period is Simone de Beauvoir's *The Second Sex* (1949), a seminal work which questions the whole position and role of woman in society. She shows how in patriarchy woman has been forced to occupy a secondary position in relation to man. She observes: "In the mouth of a man the epithet 'female' has the sound of an insult, yet he is not ashamed of his animal nature, on the contrary, he is proud if someone says to him, 'He is a male!'" (35) She believes that this secondary position is not imposed of necessity by natural "feminine" characteristics but rather by strong environmental forces of social traditions and education which have been under the control of man. Man considers himself "Subject" and "Absolute" and woman is the "Other" (Beauvoir 29).

The late 1960s witnessed an intensification of the feminist struggle in Europe and America. The movement acquired political dimensions and turned aggressive. Feminists felt that women had been poor victims of male oppression and exploitation, and expressed anger and strong resentment against injustice done to them. Betty Friedan's *The Feminine Mystique* (1963) questions the percept that a woman in a patriarchal system must remain confined to domesticity and childcare.

But soon enough the political action of the feminists was extended to the cultural field. The main task before the feminists, therefore, was to expose the patriarchal practices in literary discourse. Mary Ellman's *Thinking about Women* (1968) is a scathing analysis of the portrayal of women by women. Kate Millett's *Sexual Politics* (1969) examines how politics operate in the relationship between sexes. Millett, through her analysis of the novels of male writers like Norman Mailer and Henry Miller, exposes their patriarchal bias and their sexual/textual harassment of women. She says that the essence of politics is power and the task of feminist critics and theorists is to expose the male dominance over females.

If writers like Mary Ellman and Kate Millett have been busy "with the male discourse" or representations of women by men, the other feminist critics like Elaine Showalter, Susan Gubar and Sandra Gilbert have been preoccupied with "women's self-representation." These writers chose to express their female anger in a series of duplicitous textual strategies. Both the angel and the monster are aspects of the author's self-image. "The ideal woman is seen as a passive, docile and above all selfless creature. . . . The monster woman for Gilbert and Gubar is duplicitous, precisely because she has something to tell: there is always the possibility that she may choose not to tell—or to tell a different story." (Moi 58)

Thus, feminist criticism operates in three ways: (1) it unfolds the literary representations of sexual difference; (2) it brings out the ways that literary genres have been shaped by masculine and feminine values; (3) and it shows the exclusion of the female voice from the institutions of literature, criticism, and theory. (S. Singh 1)

Elaine Showalter in *A Literature of Their Own* discovers three major phases of historical development which she claims to be common to all literary movements: "First, there is a prolonged phase of the prevailing modes of the dominant tradition. . . . Second, there is a phase of protest against these standards. . . . Finally, there is a phase of self-discovery. . . . An appropriate terminology for women writers is to call these stages, feminine, feminist, and female." (13) She divides feminist criticism into two distinct varieties. The first is *feminist critique* concerned with woman as reader—woman as the consumer of male-produced literature. Its main concerns are the images and stereotypes of women in literature, the omissions and the misconceptions about women in criticism, and the fissures in male-constructed literary history. Then there is *gynocriticism* which is concerned with woman as writer—with woman as the producer of textual meaning. Though the *feminist critique* is essentially political and polemical, gynocriticism is more self-contained and experimental.

Another text which enjoys a privileged status in feminist circles, is *The Madwoman in the Attic* written by Sandra Gilbert and Susan Gubar. It aims to describe the "distinctively female literary tradition" (11) of the nineteenth century and to propound a complex theory of women's creativity. The authors' argument runs somewhat like this: "the nature of difference of woman's writing lies in its troubled or even tormented relationship to female identity; the woman writer experiences her own gender as 'a painful obstacle or debilitating inadequacy.' (Qtd. Moi 319) Though she possesses a distinctive female voice or power, she can give expression to it only in a roundabout or indirect manner.

Then there are feminist critics like Toril Moi and Julia Kristeva who are deconstructionists. Toril Moi in her *Sexual/ Textual Politics* (1988) insists on the necessity of deconstructing the opposition between the traditionally "masculine" and "feminine" values and to confront the full political force and reality of such categories. According to her, the very fact of being female does not necessarily guarantee a feminist approach. Works by women on women writers also do not necessarily exemplify anti-patriarchal commitment. She also distinguishes the often confused terms "feminist," "feminine," and "femaleness." "Feminism" is described as a "political situation," "femaleness" as a matter of biology and "femininity" as a set of culturally defined characteristics (Moi 65). In this usage "feminine" represents nurture and "female" nature. "Femininity," thus, is a social construct. As Simone de Beauvoir says, "one isn't born a woman, one becomes one." Patriarchal oppression imposes certain social standards of femininity on all women such as sweetness, modesty, subservience, humility etc. in order to prove that these standards of "femininity" are natural. The deconstruction of Helen Cixous shows femininity as lack, negativity, absence of meaning, irrationality, chaos and darkness. And she has disapproved of the attempts of feminists to develop another set of feminine virtues as this would just become a part of the metaphysical binary oppositions.

It is essential to clear the confusion between female and femininity. Women are female but this doesn't mean that they will be feminine. To make women believe that there is such a thing as essence of femaleness, called femininity, serves the interests of patriarchy. The French-Bulgarian linguist and psychoanalyst Julia Kristeva considers femininity as marginality. She thinks femaleness is a matter of choices, a choice between the semiotic of the mother and the symbolic of the father and not something intrinsic; it is a question of positionality, not essences. Thus, she offers a position and not a definition to femininity. She refuses to define femininity as she doesn't consider it the essence. She argues for feminist struggle to be seen historically and politically as a three-tiered phenomenon: (1) women demand equal access to the symbolic order, which is considered to be Liberal feminism; (2) women reject the male symbolic order in the name of difference, termed Radical feminism—femininity extolled; (3) women reject the dichotomy between masculine and feminine as metaphysical. She strongly advocates the third position: "What can 'identity,' even 'sexual identity,' mean in a new theoretical and scientific space where the very notion of identity is challenged?" (Kristeva 34)

Toril Moi doesn't accept this third position in its entirety because with this one loses touch with the political reality of feminism. There is still need to claim women's place in society and to emphasize the difference between male and female experience of the world. She has divided the field of feminist criticism into two main categories: (1) female criticism, and (2) feminine theory. Female criticism means criticism which in some way focuses on women authors just to judge whether their work is feminist or not. Feminine theory means the construction of femininity. Toril Moi finds the works of Freud the best illustration of theory formulation. According to her, creative transformation of psychoanalysis can effectively be used for formulating a non-essentialist theory of human sexuality and desire in order to understand the power relations between the sexes.

One charge that is often levelled against American White Feminist criticism is that it has not paid sufficient attention to the problems of class and race in addition to gender. That's why the Black Feminists have established a separate canon for themselves. In Great Britain, the Marxist Feminist critics take up the problem of class along with gender. But they, too, like their American and French counterparts, have overlooked the dimensions of race, nation, empire, etc. and have therefore been taken to task by their Third World Sisters e.g., from her site in the Western academy Chandra Talpade Mohanty reminds the First World Feminists: "Beyond sisterhood there is racism, colonialism and imperialism" (32). Thus, the problems of women in the various Third World countries may differ according to their national, historical or local contexts. Suma Chitnis in her article "Feminism: Indian Ethos and Indian Convictions" expresses "the situation of Indian women is, in many ways, worse than the situation of American and European women" (8).

One of the main reasons for the poor status of women in India is the value system by which women abide. Devotion to the husband is cultivated among girls of all religions, but it is particularly idealized and firmly institutionalized in the Hindu concept of "pativrata." The images of Sita, Savitri or Ahilaya—women known for their exceptional devotion to their husbands—still proliferate in popular media. In an article, "I'm Every Woman" in *The Indian Express*, Parul and Jaskiran Kapoor articulate: "Parenting, career, home . . . it's a tough call and a challenge that takes not just physical, but emotional toll as well. But for many women it's worth the effort and at the end of the day, there is a satisfaction of playing many roles, to perfection." (Parul 1) Media, hence, nowadays, is presenting a new concept of "Supermoms." There is now as Rajeswari Sunder Rajan calls:

"the emergence of a new Indian woman in media and official discourse in India today, a construction which serves not only to reconcile in her subjectivity the conflicts between tradition and modernity in Indian society, but works also to deny the actual conflict that women existentially register as an aspect of their lives." (129)

These new representations of women instead of doing away with gender differences and gender discriminations perpetuate them under a new guise. "Modernity, according to this version, instead of deflecting the Indian woman from her traditional roles and chores, facilitates their easy and efficient performance and thereby vindicates her Indian identity." (Palkar 24) Thus, the feminist critic in India on the one hand is trying to resist patriarchal ideologies and on the other is encouraging the kind of self-representations of women resulting in conflicts.

Sandra Gilbert and Susan Gubar in their *The Madwoman in the Attic* (1979) state: "For the female artist the essential process of self-definition is complicated by all those patriarchal definitions that intervene between herself and herself" (Qtd. Moi 58). The dire consequence of this predicament is that the woman writer inevitably comes to suffer from a debilitating anxiety of authorship. They further remark that the fundamental problem of feminine literary criticism is: "Since his is the chief voice she hears, does the queen try to sound like the king, imitating his tone, his inflections, his point of view, or does she 'talk back' to him in her own vocabulary, her own timbre, insisting on her own viewpoint?" (Qtd. Moi 59) This, they call, is "mad double" or "female schizophrenia of authorship."

Thus, there is no single feminist theory. It has several different approaches and positions like socio-economic, psychological, literary etc. However, its two primary concerns are power and freedom as these have traditionally been denied to a woman, placing them on the margins. Feminisms range from the purely rebellious stance of the shrieking, bra-burning type to the more balanced multivalent "womanist" and "humanist" and the depth, complexity and multiplicity of feminism is expressed in the following words of Robin Morgan:

> There is something every woman bears around her neck on a thin chain of fear—an amulet of madness. For each of us, there exists somewhere a moment of insult so intense that she will reach up and rip the amulet off even if the chain tears at the flesh of her neck. . . . We are rising: powerful in our unclean bodies; bright glowing mad in our inferior brains: wild hair flying, wild eyes staring, wild voices keening, . . . stuffing fingers into our mouths to stop the screams of fear and hate and pity for men we have loved and love still. (Qtd. Mathur 17)

In India this gender disparity or sex-inequality is a social reality and to understand it in the Indian situation it is important to grasp the reality in its traditional framework. Manu, whose philosophy occupies a significant place in the mainstream of Indian ideology and culture, does express some noble sentiments about women: "Where females are honoured, there the deities are pleased; but where they are dishonoured, there all religious acts become fruitless." Yet he too constantly stresses the inferiority of women to men. According to him, a wife must ever remain devoted to her husband. "Even though the husband be of bad character and seeks pleasure elsewhere he may be constantly worshipped as a god by a faithful wife" (68). In Vedas and Epics, we come across the names of learned women like Gargi, Maitreyi, Tara, Sulabha, etc. But it is doubtful whether women were accorded equal status at every level of social interaction.

"From 13th to 16thh century, the Bhakti cult flourished the ideal of equality between man and woman. . . . All were sparks of the one supreme deity" (Qtd. Bhoite 253). But still woman was considered a great obstruction in the way of spiritual realization. Eknath wrote, "An aspirant must therefore keep himself aloof from the influence of woman." Tukaram evinced a similar prejudice against women, "Give me not the company of women . . . for by them I forget God's worship and my mind goes beyond my control." Kabir called woman a "hellish well" (Qtd. Kapadia 257).

The Koran also repeatedly stresses the superiority of men over women. A woman's function in life is to provide the male with sexual gratification and progeny. The Koran says: "Men are superior to women on account of the qualities with which God had gifted the one above the other. . . . Virtuous women are obedient, careful during the husband's absence because God hath on them been careful." (415) A Jew made his morning prayer in the following manner: "Blessed be God . . . that He did not make me a woman" (Beauvoir 22). Buddhism also does not have much to say in favour of women. According to Buddhists, the company of woman was considered to be an obstacle in the development of higher powers in man. The Buddha tells his disciple:

> Women are soon angered, Ananda,
> Women are full of passion, Ananda,
> Women are envious, Ananda,
> Women are stupid. (Qtd. Kidwai 14)

In the colonial period, there were several reformers who started questioning the subordinate position of woman in Indian society. With Raja Rammohun Roy many other social ameliorates came forward to annihilate injustice meted out to a woman. They tackled such issues as Sati, fate of widow, widow remarriage, polygamy, child-marriage, denial of property rights and education to woman. They thought that removal of these disabilities would pave the way for equality between the sexes. Though such social reform movements of the 19th century and the nationalist movement of 20th century helped a lot in improving the condition of an Indian woman yet "for society as a whole, sex roles, stereotype images and the Indian woman's conception of herself and her role in life remained virtually unchanged" (Agnew 61).

On January 18, 1900 Vivekananda at the Shakespeare Club in Pasadena, California, was questioned about women of India. He referred to his inadequate knowledge of women of India—of their relation, of different languages and dialects that Indian women speak, of their race and castes and also of their manners and customs. Thus, he spoke of the ideal of Indian women. From the feminist angle with reference to Indian situation, only a woman knows what she experiences, so only she can speak of it. Everybody lives his or her life individually and differently. Pain differs from person to person. Nobody can speak for anybody. The reality of the situation is that in Indian situation, a woman in general, still retains the required patience and courage to avoid any disequilibrium in the family relationship and this relationship remains maintained only through her subordination by man. Family still exists in India despite many blows to it and the credit for it goes to Indian woman. In the West, the only effective relationship is that of husband and wife. That too, till it lasts. In India other relationships like brother-sister relationship and the relationship of children with their grandparents are also very strong and concrete.

The media is also responsible for projecting the image of woman in a distorted manner. She is portrayed as sexy, glamorous and frivolous. Indian films, too, preach feminine values of submission, devotion and self-sacrifice. The attitude of the press and media towards distressed woman is rather unhealthy and quite unsympathetic, and these often present cases of rape etc. as spicy stories. Vrinda Nabar has listed various factors—caste, class, economic deprivation, sectarian fragmentation, size and numbers, overpopulation, the growing power of fundamental forces, the sway of superstitions, female foeticide and above all the essential nature of what she terms as Hinduism—that create vastly different scenario in India encompassing contradictions of a kind undreamed of in mainstream (Western) feminist philosophy.

Thus an overview of the entire span of more than two centuries reveals that woman has always been at the receiving end in India. Even in the present times the lot of an economically independent woman is no better. She has to perform double duties.

She is never thought of as an independent individual taking her own decisions.

> Never the state nor the organization raised the fundamental questions basic to gender inequality, whenever some problems such as unequal sex-ratio etc., come on the surface certain laws were made to mitigate the evil. But the basic issues were never questioned. (Bhoite 255)

However, in the changing pattern of society, because of the spread of industrialization, new scientific invention, rapid spread of education, a woman—particularly the educated one—has started feeling the uneasy burden of suppression or subjugation. She has become vocal in defining her identity as she is likely to be influenced by the changing attitude of the civilization as a whole. "It's heartening to see that women are realizing their worth and there is no moral pressure to continue in a relationship because it is considered virtuous. A woman today is multi-faceted; her identity is no longer linked with the man she's with." (Varma 1)

But at the same time the social perception goes on hammering into her unconscious, weighing her down mentally. She experiences a conflict between her personal values and larger social practices. The cultural and social assumptions prevent her from making contact with her own self. And this has resulted in her schizophrenic tendency. A woman in general feels insecure; she feels at times asphyxiated amid the male-dominance. In his book *The Divided Self*, R.D. Laing proposes: "our sense of ontological security is a prerequisite for psychological health and that many instances of mental illness are primarily a result of a lack in basic security of the self." (1)

A woman in India faces utter humiliation when the dowry system impinges on her psychic make-up. "Indian woman caught in the flux of tradition and modernity saddled with the burden of past but both to cast off her aspirations (sic) . . . constitutes the crux of feminism in Indian literature." (Bhatnagar 1) Her psyche keeps being visited by alternate moods of hope and despair, of glow and gloom in her odyssey for identity and freedom. Women "have very limited freedom. . . . Either society, religion or tradition control them and more often than not religion, tradition and morality are used to exclude women from power and knowledge and reinforce patriarchal authority" (Jain 84).

Simone de Beauvoir in *The Second Sex* expresses: "the drama of woman lies in a conflict between the fundamental aspirations of every subject (ego)—who always regards the self as the essential—and the compulsions of a situation in which she is the inessential. How can a human being in woman's situation attain fulfillment?" (Beauvoir 29) She contends against Freud and the theoretical precepts of psychoanalysis as it assumes an original superiority of the male. Her main objection is to the male bias: "Freud writes—'the libido is constantly and regularly male in essence, whether it appears in man or a woman'" (Beauvoir 71). It is difficult to apply Kate Millett or Simone de Beauvoir or whoever to the reality of Indian life as there are such terrible misconceptions about feminism by people here. Here in India, it is often considered that feminism is something about bra-burning and breaking away relations with husband and children, or about not being married, not having children, etc. "I actually feel that a lot of women in India are feminists without knowing it" (A. Singh 129).

The agonies of a woman ultimately result in her bewilderment and sense of rootlessness. Her dislocated mind suffers the nightmares of shut-in-life and appears schizophrenic.

> As a child a girl identifies herself with her father, then she becomes possessed with a feeling of inferiority with reference to the male and is faced with a dilemma: either to assert her independence and become virilized—which, with the underlying complex of inferiority induces a state of tension that threatens neurosis—or to find happy fulfillment in amorous submission. (Beauvoir 75)

True emotional satisfaction has always eluded the psyche of a woman. The acceptance or rejection, denial or disapproval at the emotional level creates in her inner storm, a mutiny within. She is always "hesitating between the role of object, Other which is offered her, and the assertion of her liberty" (Beauvoir 77).

Psychoanalytical theories are important in understanding the subjugation of women in patriarchy. They tell us how this process of "becoming" a woman actually occurs. They explore how it is that a woman can come to identify with patriarchal interests, and set about answering this question by investigating the unconscious structure of gender identity. Initially these theories were rejected by the feminists like Simone de Beauvoir, Kate Millett, Betty Friedan etc. The principle cause of rejection was Freud's concept of "penis envy" and statement "anatomy is destiny" which he used to define woman's relationship to language, fantasy and culture.

In her path-breaking *The Feminine Mystique*, Betty Friedan denounces Freud, claiming that his theories sound a single, overprotective, life-restricting, future-denying note for women. Four major texts appeared in 1970-1971 alone, each indicting Freud for the crime of misogyny. Kate Millett in *Sexual Politics* names Freud "the strongest individual counter-revolutionary force in the ideology of sexual politics"; Shulamith Firestone in *The Dialectic of Sex* refers contemptuously to Freudianism as "our modern Church"; Eva Figes in *Patriarchal Attitudes* describes Freudian psychoanalysis as "a magic formula more powerful than any fence"; and Germaine Greer in *The Female Eunuch* dismisses it cavalierly as "nonsense."

Kate Millett notes that the bulk of Freud's essays on femininity appeared in the early twentieth century amid the sexual revolution and the rise of feminism. Freud shaped his arguments directly in response to these challenges and, Millett emphasizes, "conceded nothing." Firestone agrees, identifying Freudianism as an ideological backlash to the first stirring of women's emancipation. Freud is, Ellen Frankfort contends in *Vaginal Politics* (1972), "the product of a repressed Victorian upbringing and an authoritarian education" (Qtd. Buhle 233).

Horney also believed that Anatomy is not Destiny. Contrary to Sigmund Freud, the Oedipal Complex does not apply to most men and to no women. Penis envy, to her, was not really envying the penis in its literal sense, but envying men's social status and role. She believes that there is something wrong with society and not women.

However, when the search for the cause of women's oppression did not end, a feminist reassessment of psychoanalysis began as it helped in grasping the interior dimensions of this oppression. The feminists yielded to the sweeping influence of psychoanalysis as an explanatory philosophy. Feminist theorists such as Juliet Mitchell, Nancy Chodorow, Jessica Benjamin, Jane Gallop and Jane Flax argued that Freud and various psychoanalytic theories are essentially related to the feminist project. Though Freud didn't write much on women, femininity or female sexuality except in his three major essays: "Some Psychical Consequences of Anatomical Distinction between the Sexes" (1925), "Female Sexuality" (1931) and "Femininity" (1933), but he and his psychoanalytical theories, especially the theory of the Oedipal stage of psychosexual development, have remained prominent concerns among feminists.

Freud's theoretical assumption is that psychosexual development follows an identical route in both the sexes up to a certain age after which the paths diverge. Normally the boy ends up being masculine and the girl feminine. At the centre of this theory of childhood development is the Oedipus complex. According to Freud, a boy's close relation to his mother, as the primary love-object, leads to a desire for complete union with her. Later on, he abandons this incestuous desire out of fear of being castrated by his father. The Oedipal crisis for a boy comes about when he discovers that he is different from his mother (he has a penis) but he is the same as his father. His mother is perceived as castrated through her lack of a penis and this symbolizes the inferiority of the feminine as the boy adjusts to the reality principle, and waits for the day when he will be the patriarch. In this way the boy develops both a superego and an id and identifies with his father and the symbolic role of manhood.

The girl's route through the Oedipal stage is far more problematic in Freud's view. "Realizing" that she is castrated and thus inferior, the girl turns away from her similarly castrated mother and attempts to "seduce" her father. When this fails, she returns to the mother and identifies with her feminine role. However, she still envies the penis.

> This places the girl in a position of ambivalence where she belongs completely to neither the mother nor the father but still seeks to belong to the powerful masculine culture. (Madsen 95)

According to theorists like Nancy Chodorow, as a consequence of this psychosexual development girls are less individuated than boys, with more fluid ego boundaries. So gender identity is much less secure for girls than for boys after the Oedipal stage.

Instead of Oedipus complex as a symmetric structure it is an asymmetric one in which both the infants love their mother and abandon her at the intervention of the father.

> boy learns to accept his inferior phallic powers (thus resolving his castration complex) but on understanding that he will later have the same patriarchal rights and a woman of his own; the girl learns that she has no phallic powers . . . indeed that she is like her mother, without the phallus: she recognizes her castration, envies the phallic power, and has to do her best to overcome this envy. [Freud uses the term "penis-envy" and this has produced a misleadingly biological interpretation.] (Mitchell 230)

A sense of inferiority closely connected therewith, a repression of masturbation, sets her on the path towards femininity and this is the triumph of her feminine destiny under patriarchy.

> If we might elaborate on Freud here, we could say that where the boy's resolution and abandonment of his Oedipus complex is his entry into his cultural heritage, the girl, on the contrary, finds her cultural place in patriarchal society. (Mitchell 231)

Sexuality and Unconscious, the two pillars of psychoanalysis, are responsible for people's behaviour and their mental lives. Sexuality is not a fixed entity. It is a consequence of a long and tortuous process of development. The unconscious is a reservoir of the repressed, the repressed which can be glimpsed in dreams, jokes, slips of the tongue etc. Problems stem from cultural restrictions on sexual expression. Unacceptable sexual wishes are repressed into the "System Unconscious" and this repression creates anxiety. Often, dreams give clues to unconscious conflicts, and for this reason, Freud refers to dreams as the "royal road to the Unconscious." Freud's structural theory in a small book called *The Ego and the Id* explains the cause of neurotic symptoms like phobias, compulsions, obsessions, depressions, and "hysterical" conversions. Such problems according to him are created by intrapsychic conflicts i.e. the conflicts among various wishes and the sense of guilt, which ultimately produce anxiety, depression and anger. Super-ego which is a symbolic internalization of the father figure and cultural regulations is constantly watching each one of the ego's moves and punishes it with inferiority.

In the articles which run from 1924 to 1931, Freud also moves from that famous, or rather infamous, description of the little girl struck with her "inferiority" or "injury" in the face of the anatomy of the little boy and wisely accepting her fate, to the account which quite explicitly describes the process of becoming "feminine" as an "injury" or "catastrophe" for the complexity of her earlier psychic and sexual life. Thus, Freud and his psychoanalysis is the key to understand the oppression of women under patriarchy.

> When everyone conceived of people as individually responsible for their actions, he [Freud] showed the impact of society. When everyone thought of male and female as roles determined by nature or God, he showed how much they depended on family dynamics. (Boeree 16)

Later on, Jacques Lacan dedicated himself to re-defining and re-formulating the work of Sigmund Freud in linguistic and structuralistic terms. In agreement with Freud, Lacan stressed that both sexuality and unconscious cannot in any degree be pre-given facts, they are constructions. He interpreted Freud's theories in the light of Saussurian linguistics and tried to find out the ways in which human subject is constructed. According to him, the human subject is constructed within the terms of language. Language doesn't arise from within the individual, it is always out there in the world outside. Thus, the 'I' and 'me' of the human baby don't come from within but from elsewhere.

Like Freud, Lacan discusses the importance of the pre-Oedipal stage in the child's life and refers to this stage as the Imaginary. He theorizes that the acquisition of language and its entry into its Symbolic Order occurs at the Oedipal phase in which the child accepts his or her gender identity. However, there occurs a loss of primal, maternal identification with the world. This lack is repressed and creates unconscious which does not remain entirely repressed but erupts into language, creating meaningless, contradictory expressions. All human society and culture is dominated by the Symbolic Order which itself represents a lack, the loss of the unity of the Imaginary Order. The Imaginary is gendered by its close association with the mother; the Symbolic is the realm of the father: the public, objective world of language and reason and social relations.

Thus, the Oedipal crisis brings about the perception of difference between self and Other, and a fundamental element of the entry into the post-Oedipal or "Symbolic Order" is the acquisition of the father's language. This stage leads to an acceptance of the phallus as a privileged signification and a consequent female displacement and neurosis. Mother and Father; pre-Oedipal and post-Oedipal stages; Imaginary and Symbolic Orders; primal and civilized identities; nature and culture; psychosis and rationality—these oppositions structure the process whereby individuals are initiated into human society and acquire gender identities, language, social relationships, and the like. In other words, this is the process which leads a woman to inferior and subordinate position.

Carl Jung, another psychoanalyst, views every individual as both feminine and masculine. According to him, each of us has all human qualities, by virtue of our common human heritage; personality development requires recognizing and dealing with all aspects of our personality. The problem is that social experiences are likely to encourage the development of only one set of characteristics and discourage the development of the other. We are thus often led to "forget who we really are." We are encouraged to think of ourselves only in terms of what we consciously develop and show to the world as our outer character—the mask that Jung calls the persona. The persona is feminine or masculine, and whatever qualities are lacking in this outer character are present in the inner character, or the soul. "The unrecognized inner characteristics may influence our behaviour in unusual ways" (Donelson 26). His theory of neurosis is also beneficial in understanding a woman's psyche as it is related to tensions between various opposite attitudes in a self-regulating dynamic. The ego, being the centre of consciousness, represents the coalescing attitude of consciousness. The ego's attitude is in tension with a complementary and balancing attitude in the unconscious. However, he considers the divided psyche normal as it is an undeniable common inheritance of all mankind.

Alfred Adler, along with Freud and Jung, is also considered to be one of the three founding figures of depth psychology, which emphasizes the unconscious and psychodynamics. He also argues in favour of feminism making the case that power dynamics between men and women (and associations with masculinity and femininity) are crucial to understanding human psychology. He believes that feelings of superiority and inferiority were often gendered and expressed symptomatically in characteristic masculine and feminine styles. These styles could form the basis of psychic compensation and lead to mental health difficulties.

Carl Rogers' theory is also relevant to our concerns, though he did not discuss sex similarities and differences in the detail of Freud and Jung. Like Jung, Rogers notes that the social experiences interfere with growth by inhibiting the recognition of one's potentialities.

Anna Freud also contributed to the understanding of anxiety and depression. She moved away from the classical position of her father, who was concentrating on the unconscious id (a perspective she found to be restrictive) and instead emphasized the importance of the ego, the constant struggle and conflict it experiences due to the need to fulfil contradictory wishes, desires, values and demands of reality. In this her arguments come closer to the discussion undertaken at hand as an attempt is being made to reflect a similar conflict in contemporary Indian women's poetry in English.

Nancy Chodorow in her *The Reproduction of Mothering: Psychoanalysis and the Sociology of Gender* (1978) revises traditional psychoanalytic concepts. Using Freudian psychoanalytic theory, she has argued that young girls remain mother-identified even after the Oedipus complex symbolically separates the male child from his mother. Chodorow believes that the acceptance of the domestic ideal is the foundation of women's oppression. She begins with Freud's assertion that the individual is born bisexual and that the child's mother is its first sexual object. However, the male child easily identifies with the agency and freedom of the father and emulates his possessive interest in the mother/wife. This task is not as simple for the female child. The mother identifies with her more strongly, and the daughter attempts to make the father her new love object and remains caught in a libidinal triangle where the ego is pulled among love for the father, the love of the mother, and concern and worry over the relationship of the father to the mother. Thus, according to her, "women's difficulties come after the Oedipal phase, in which male power and cultural hegemony give sex differences a transformed value" (Qtd. Showalter, *Feminist* 320).

Another feminist who finds potential worth in the use of Freud's theories for the feminist movement is Shulamith Firestone. In "Freudianism: The Misguided Feminism", she discusses how Freudianism is essentially completely accurate, with the exception of one crucial detail: everywhere that Freud writes "penis", the word should be replaced with "power." In *The Dialectic of Sex* (1970) she reads the history of "first-wave" feminism as a battle with what she calls "Freudianism"; feminism, she argues lost the battle.

Jacqueline Rose in her "Femininity and its Discontents" says: "Feminism's affinity with psychoanalysis rests above all, with this recognition there is a resistance to identity at the very heart of psychic life" (Qtd. Mitchell 354). The conflict between stereotype roles enforced on a woman and her feminist desires leads her to frustration—the frustration which leaves a permanent sting on her soul—taking her to the verge of schizophrenia.

> Hysteria is the woman's simultaneous acceptance and refusal of the organization of sexuality under patriarchal capitalism. It is simultaneously what woman can do both to be feminine and to refuse femininity within patriarchal discourse. (Mitchell 427)

The same is the case with contemporary Indian women poets. Their preoccupation with the conflicting aspects of life needs serious consideration.

> Although women today are becoming economically independent and are educationally and occupationally mobile, we can still safely compare their emotional world to that of Sita. (R. Singh 126)

The lives of women revolve around the pivot of marriage. A heavy pressure is exerted by the society on the women to pull on their marriage even if it is disintegrating. Male chauvinism has been taken for granted through the entire course of human evolution. If women have ever raised the question of the position of men in the society, the theme of sacrifice is dinned into their supple minds resulting in their divided selves and schizophrenia.

Clinically speaking, "the schizophrenias are a group of psychotic disorders characterized mainly by gross distortions of reality; withdrawal from social interaction; and disorganization and fragmentation of perception, thought and emotion." (Carson 427) These are a state of mental impairments which result in frustration and depression. Suspicious and frightened, the victim fears he can trust neither his own senses, nor the motives of other people. "With the schizophrenias, we move into a realm of behavioral disorder that represent in many ways ultimate in psychological breakdown" (Carson 427-28).

The psychoanalytical feminist approach can be very helpful in analyzing the schizophrenic tendencies of the poets taken for study. It will also help in understanding why the poems of these poets are mostly gender-inflicted narratives of suppression and exclusion and why the poetry written by them is the "poetry of memory, dreams, anxieties, fears and self-revelations" (King 133). In all the seven poets selected for study, this psychoanalytical feminist perspective can assist in assessing the ambivalence between the tendency to rebel and to conform in conventional woman and the resultant schizophrenic tendency.

All this doesn't mean that these poets are clinically neurotic. Graziano in his essay "Poetry Writing Therapy and Schizophrenia: A Poet's Point of View" says: "an oscillation between regression and full vigilance . . . results in a creative product" (51). According to him, a poet has the ability to move "back and forth" over the repressive barriers, "in and out" of the unconscious—to regress in service of the ego. If he can enter the unconscious at will, and withdraw and enter again, and again withdraw, and with the logical \ rational functions of the secondary processes organize and utilize this material then it can be said that he is "using 'in and out' route of the unconscious and he has the ability to use primary process material in service of the ego" (51).

Vacillating between passivity and rebellion, the contemporary Indian women poets get frustrated and disappointed. Their unusual tearfulness, deep sadness, suicidal attempts, delusions, hallucinations, disorderly thinking can be compared with the condition of those who lead a schizophrenic existence.

Works Cited

Agnew, Vijay. *Elite Women in Indian Politics*. New Delhi: Vikas, 1979.

Beauvoir, Simone de. *The Second Sex*. Trans. H.M. Parshley. New York: Vintage, 1952.

Bhatnagar, O.P. "Feminist English Literature—An Introduction." *Feminist English Literature*. Ed. Manmohan K. Bhatnagar. New Delhi: Atlantic, 1999. 1-9.

Bhoite, Anuradha. "Feminist Perspectives: Some Thoughts (Approaches to Gender Disparities in India)." *Contemporary Indian Women: Collected Works*. Vol. 6. Ed. Dharam Vir and Kamlesh Mahajan. New Delhi: New Academic, 1996. 249-58.

Boeree, C. George. "Freud and Psychoanalysis." 22 April 2008 <webspace.ship.edu/cgboer/psychoanalysis.html>.

Buhle, Mari Jo. *Feminism and its Discontents: A Century of Struggle with Psychoanalysis*. Cambridge: Harvard UP, 1998.

Carson, Robert C., and James N. Butcher. *Abnormal Psychology and Modern Life*. 9th ed. New York: Harper Collins, 1992.

Chitnis, Suma. "Feminism: Indian Ethos and Indian Convictions." *Feminism in India*. Ed. Maitrayee Chaudhuri. New Delhi: Kali for Women, 2004. 8-25.

Crawford, Mary, and Rhoda Unger. *Women and Gender: A Feminist Psychology*. Boston: McGraw Hill, 2000.

Donelson, Elain, and Jeanne E. Gullahorn. *Woman: A Psychological Perspective*. New York: John Wiley, 1977.

Freud, Sigmund. *The Interpretation of Dreams*. Vol. 4. London: Penguin, 1991.

Gibbs, Nancy. "The War against Feminism." *Time*. March 1992, 42-43.

Gilbert, Sandra, and Susan Gubar. *The Madwoman in the Attic: The Woman Writer and the Nineteenth-Century Literary Imagination*. London: Yale University Press, 1979.

Graziano, Frank. "Poetry Writing Therapy and Schizophrenia: A Poet's Point of View." *Literature and Psychology* 29.1 (1979): 49-59.

Jain, Jasbir. "Positioning the 'Post' in Post-Feminism: Reworking the Strategies." *Indian Feminism*. Creative New Lit. Ser. 51. Ed. Jasbir Jain and Avadhesh Kumar Singh. New Delhi: Creative, 2001. 80-95.

Kapadia, K.M. *Marriage and Family in India*. Bombay: Oxford UP, 1958.

Kidwai, Shaikh M.H. *Woman*. Delhi: Seema, 1976.

Kristeva, Julia. "Women's Times." *Signs* 7:1 (1981): 13-35.

Laing, R.D. "Divided Selves." 23 May 2008 <www.jesslayton.com/ jessweb/Essays/Ontological%20Insecurity%20-%201995.pdf>.

Madsen, Deborah L. *Feminist Theory and Literary Practice*. London: Pluto Press, 2000.

Manu. *Manusmriti*, 111, 56, in Manav Dharma Shastra. Vol. 3. Ed. and trans. Graves Haughton Chamnen. New Delhi: Cosmo, 1982.

Mathur, O.P. "Shelley's Beatrice Cenci: Feminity and Feminism." *Feminism and Literature: New Point of View*. Ed. K.K. Sharma. New Delhi: K.K. Publications, 1996. 17-26.

Mitchell, Juliet. "Femininity, narrative and psychoanalysis." *Modern Criticism and Theory*. Ed. David Lodge. Delhi: Pearson, 1988. 307-30.

Mohanty, Chandra Talpade. "Under Western Eyes: Feminist Scholarship and Colonial Discourses." *Feminism without Borders: Decolonising Theory, Practising Solidarity*. New Delhi: Duke UP, 2003. 17-42.

_____. "Under Western Eyes: Feminist Scholarship and Colonial Discourses." 16 April 2008 <www.stumptuous.com/ comps/mohanty.html>.

Moi, Toril. *Sexual/Textual Politics: Feminist Literary Theory*. 2nd ed. London: Routledge, 1988.

Palkar, Sarla. "Feminist Literary Theory: Creating New Maps." *Women's Writing: Text and Context*. Ed. Jasbir Jain. Jaipur: Rawat, 1966. 12-27.

Parul, and Jaskiran Kapoor. "I'm Every Woman: The Supermoms' Diary." *The Indian Express* 10 May 2008, Panchkula: 1.

Rajan, Rajeswari Sunder. *Real and Imagined Women: Gender, Culture and Postcolonialism*. London: Routledge, 1993.

Sharma, K.K. "Feminism: Some Observations." *Feminism and Literature: New Point of View*. Ed. K.K. Sharma. Delhi: K.K. Publications, 1996. 189-204.

Showalter, Elaine. "Feminist Criticism in the Wilderness." *Modern Criticism and Theory*. Ed. David Lodge. Delhi: Pearson Education, 1988. 307-30.

_____. *A Literature of Their Own*. Princeton: Princeton UP, 1977.

Singh, Avadhesh Kumar. "Self or Motherhood: Is that the Question?" *Indian Feminism*. Ed. Jasbir Jain and Avadhesh Kumar Singh. New Delhi: Creative, 2001. 118-32.

Singh, Renuka. *The Womb of Mind: A Sociological Exploration of the Status Experience of Women in Delhi*. New Delhi: Vikas, 1990.

Singh, Sushila. "Outlining Feminist Literary Criticism: Woman as Reader/Writer Perspective." *Feminism and Literature: New Point of View*. Ed. K.K. Sharma. Delhi: K.K. Publications, 1996. 1-9.

Steinem, Gloria. "interesting, miscellaneous, writings and quotations." 27 May 2008 <http://www.paxworks.com/miscquotes.html>.

The Koran. Trans. J.M. Rodwell. Hertz: Everyman's Library, 1909.

Varma, Anuradha. "It's a Woman's World." Times Life. *Sunday Times of India* April 27, 2008.

Poetic Manifestations of Schizophrenic Experience

Society demands mute acceptance from a woman. She cannot even cry. Her crying is considered her rebellion. Even her tears are intolerable, for they scare man and man begins to torture and suppress what scares him. A woman, as a result, does not have many options to exercise. She can only accept the patriarchal structures and play her roles as daughter, sister, wife and mother. Her womb further complicates her dilemma. In the process, she accepts her patriarchal tyranny and hinders her self-realization. In such a society "images and expressions like 'entrapment,' 'hysteria,' 'madness,' 'exile,' and 'isolation,'" which could be considered as "distinctive female forms," become "relevant to our understanding of the new woman" (Sheshadri xi). The same characteristics are also there in the contemporary Indian English women poets. According to Mary Eagleton, "I do not believe there is such a thing as female writing, a 'woman's voice.' There is the hysteric's voice" as the woman writer "both refuses and is totally trapped within femininity" (Eagleton 155).

Vacillating between their feminist desires on one side and their stereotyped social roles on the other, the poems of contemporary Indian English women poets are constructed differently as compared to the poems of the male writers. The dualities within these women poets leave them sad, lonely, frustrated, disappointed and empty. As it has been noted earlier their unusual tearfulness, deep sadness, suicidal attempts, delusions, hallucinations, disorderly thinking can be compared with the condition of those who lead a schizophrenic existence. These poets "map a psychology of contradictions, humiliations and defeats rather than self-assertions and triumphs" (King 133).

Schizophrenics are often compared with persons who possess a dual personality and this duality of existence is clearly evident in the poetry of contemporary Indian English women poets in which they reflect the conflict of their instincts with the reality.

> Thus, the loneliness of the female artist, her feelings of alienation from male predecessors coupled with her need for sisterly precursors and successors, her urgent sense of the need for a female audience together with her fear of the antagonism of male readers, her culturally conditioned timidity about self-dramatization, her dread of the patriarchal authority of art, her anxiety about the impropriety of female invention—all these phenomena of 'inferiorization' mark the woman writer's struggle for artistic self-definition and differentiate her efforts at self-creation from those of her male counterparts. (Gilbert 50)

All the seven poets taken for study exhibit the symptoms of schizophrenia.

The frustration and disgust with the existing reality, and the mounting desire for autonomy forces Mamta Kalia, a noteworthy Indian woman poet, to embark on a quest or a search for an identity. According to Simone de Beauvoir: "A woman's personality within her home gives her no autonomy, it is not directly useful to society, it does not open out in the future and it produces nothing" (475). This dissatisfaction results in a sense of nothingness in Mamta Kalia about which she ironically remarks:

> But nothing ever happened to me
> except two children
> and two miscarriages. ("Sheer Good Luck" 15-17)

A lack of interest and pleasure in life coupled with a feeling that things are not worth the effort because they give no pleasure is visible in the works of contemporary women poets. Mamta Kalia's poetry reflects this schizophrenic tendency through its demonstration of bizarre behaviour, disordered thinking, and reduction in emotional expressiveness of a woman. The physical relationship with her husband makes her behave eccentrically:

> Let's not come close during intercourse
> But mark a distance,
> Touch each other like dead-wire
> And react like fools. ("Come" 5-8)

As a result of social pressures which mould the very thinking of a girl and make her non-communicative about her real needs and desires, the poems constructed by these women poets reveal their "purely subjective eccentricities" (de Souza 84):

> I want to pay Sunday visits
> totally undressed ("Compulsions" 9-10)

A sense of dissatisfaction is always there in Mamta Kalia's expression and her impatience with the social etiquettes, and rebellious desire for natural life are clearly expressed:

> I want to pick my nose
> in a public place
> I want to sit in my office chair
> with my feet up. ("Compulsions" 1-4)

In her poem "Tribute to Papa" one can read between the lines Virginia Woolf's well-known phrase—"killing the angel in the house" as when she says:

> Who wants to be an angel like you? (3)

Mamta Kalia questions her father's concern about uprightness and integrity. In her efforts to pour scorn on her father's emphasis on these qualities, she exhibits an erratic behaviour.

It is the poetry concerned with personal matters and relationships, of private fears and dreams which lead to the ultimate resilience in the face of any relationship that threatens to devastate her vital and potential self. She has got registered for Ph.D. and her disillusionment is quite obvious in the following lines:

> I'm working for a Ph.D. these days.
> Even if I know

I'll never complete the thesis,
never mind,
that I'm registered is enough. ("Dedicated Teachers" 5-9)

One of the features of schizophrenia—i.e. the delusion of persecution (in which a person thinks that other persons are plotting against him)—is clearly visible in Mamta Kalia's poetry. In a personal interview, she says that when she was working in S.N.D.T. University, "my roommate used to spy on me all the time. She used to read all my letters. She used to steal my things, even bread." All this reflects the poet's desire for privacy and freedom and disappointment with the kind of life she had been made to live. She further says:

> I wanted to bite everybody. . . . I wanted to go away. I didn't know even what I wanted to do. (Kalia)

Society has a deadening effect on her because she remains torn between her own desires and expectations of the society. She could not bite, that's why, she started writing:

In my hour of discontent
I neither shout nor rant.
I simply fill ink in my pen
And spill it with intent. ("In My Hour of Discontent" 1-4)

All the time the poet remains occupied with fear which results from her non-conformity. Talking about this fear of a woman in her daily life, Doris Lessing says that it is the "fear of what other people might say, fear of being different, fear of being isolated, fear of the herd we belong to, fear of seclusion from the herd we belong to" (524).

She doesn't like to be treated as a mere object of enjoyment, nor as a domesticated servant looking after the husband, kids and kitchen, but as an independent, vivacious individual. A pervasive gloom and loneliness haunt her day in and day out. In her poem "Seize the Day" she expresses the monotony and drudgery of daily routine which seems to end in nothingness:

Days stubbed in the ash-tray
Days devoid of everything. (1-2)

It is really depressing to live through

Days of dissociation
When meanings are uprooted
And nothing endures (8-10)

Every relationship in her life has however succeeded in intensifying the crisis of disappointment. Filled with a sense of utter disgust and disappointment, she turns to poetry, "Instead of fighting, I started writing" (Interview with Eunice de Souza 58). Crammed with much torture and anguish within, Mamta Kalia finds the modern world an emotionless, arid land where all warmth and compassion have dried up. She epitomizes the state:

I have two younger brothers who call me *tayee,*
I am my mother's pet,
I am, I am.
But who will hear if I say all this?
In this large unfriendly town
Who will say, "Don't cry." ("Self-Pity" 15-20)

Outside home in the professional sphere a woman is asked to make compromises with the patriarchal regulations which lead to nervous-wrecking impact on her:

> A woman is not allowed to do something positive in her work and in consequence win recognition as a complete person. However, respected she may be she is subordinate, secondary and parasitic. (Beauvoir 475)

Mamta Kalia after facing a number of problems in her job now decides to "have it all evened up" (35) with her boss. In an unusual manner she says:

I'll hit you!
I'll tear you up! . . .
let you taste the whole of death
gradually,
as I tasted it for twenty-three years. ("Tit for Tat" 1-2, 7-9)

A very bizarre characteristic of these contemporary women poets is that though disgusted with this male-dominated world, they seem to find pleasure and contentment in man's love. In "Love Cure" Mamta Kalia writes the lover's name on her palm and her loneliness stands diminished. She aspires for a Brave New World where she hopes to meet her Prince Debonair.

This contradiction in speech and behaviour is one of the symptoms of schizophrenia and in her case it is the society which is responsible for this deadening effect. She realizes that a failure to act according to the values of conventional society can result in confusion, isolation or even madness.

Gauri Deshpande is almost exclusively concerned with man-woman relationship. She has suffered the crisis of self which emanates from her essentially occupied psyche with fears and doubts. Her poems project the crucial struggle of the psyche to overcome the tensions at different stages of her relationship with man:

> When you left me lying . .
> I hated the cold air
> drying my sweat on your hands
> and driving my thought
> from your tired thigh. ("Poems on a Lost Love" 1, 5-8)

In the article "Modern Indian English Women Poets: An Overview" Sunanda P. Chavan studies Gauri Deshpande's frustrations and dissatisfactions and attempts to trace the causes that lead to trauma. According to Chavan, her poetry gives place to sheer sentimental outbursts when the poet "abandons herself weakly to the passion of grief in the face of the traumatic experience of frustration" (*Modern* 79). As when she speaks of:

> and the now familiar beat of
> I wont cry I wont cry
> drums at the base of my throat ("Do I think of You" 10-12)

The expression is "too sentimental to be poetically valid" (Chavan, *Modern* 79) and hence, schizophrenic.

The intensity of her passion often cripples her power of exploration. Love and sex provide no enjoyment. Sex seems to her a mere dry activity that leaves women dissatisfied as men do not penetrate into the "plunging depths" of their "souls/ and bodies" ("No More" 3-4). However, at the same time Gauri Deshpande expresses her desire for man's love in some of her poems. In "Integration," tortured by the agony of existence, she longs for a lover:

> if only there were someone to fall in love with. (8)

In "Known is this City" she can tolerate the strange city "Only because we were here once, in love" (11). But soon the mood deserts her and she is found "lamenting her loneliness and emptiness" (Dwivedi 235) in her next poem at the loss of her love:

> I wanted to weep for you
> And me
> But I had already spent
> All tears in useless mournings.
> So now I watch arid-eyed
> As my fingers open slowly.
> And let you go. ("I Wanted to Weep" 1-7)

Her lost love makes her feel confused and withdrawn. Frustration and depression can be seen in her poetry now and again. She acquires a somewhat sentimental outlook:

> And as the clouds heap and heap upon the west
> I lie empty, barren and bereft. ("The Guest" 11-12)

The painful memories of love depress her and make her cheerless. The reminiscences of her lost love and the attitude of the society make her behaviour peculiar:

> Taught me carefully to read contempt
> In other faces, making me adept
> At acceptance and regret
> So now I reawait
> Like a recurrent fulfillment
> Of promise:

Your loss. ("When You Divided" 10-16)

She longs for some peace. She is tired of the unrest of her life which gives her pain and suffering:

This gnawing unrest that was sent
From far away mysteriously. . . .
Destroying to elemental everything
All that I call me. ("Integration"16-17, 19-20)

In her poem "The Female of the Species" Gauri Deshpande's behaviour becomes very peculiar as she wants to speak about love, despair and about "ungrateful" (17) children but she speaks something else which has no link with those:

Sometimes you want to talk
about love and despair
and the ungratefulness of children . . .
and speak of the rate of rice
and the price of tea
and the scarcity of cheese.
You know both that you've spoken
of love and despair and ungrateful children. (1-3, 13-17)

Logically, the topics of conversation, the price of tea, the scarcity of cheese, have nothing to do with what the speaker desires to communicate—love and despair and ungrateful children. However, by making such a comparison the poet tries to lay emphasis on the frustration experienced by women in every sphere—their dissatisfaction with relationships which is accentuated by their discussion of the material world.

To Gauri Deshpande, husband's love also doesn't seem to provide any satisfaction and it is her intense desire to be with the lover that makes her seem schizophrenic:

I walked home that evening
My shadow tossed back
and forth between the lampposts
I reached home late, he waited anxiously.
'What's the matter? Why do you look like that?
What 'that' was I never knew. ("Poems in Winter" 47-52)

She even doesn't like her child to be born with her husband's features and imagines her lover's "smoky blue eyes and golden hair" instead:

> I wished upon my child
> That is born with her father's face. (*Ibid.* 35-36)

The longing in her heart for the man who might have been her lover makes her feel confused and restless. All the moments the man who is not with her haunts her mind. The sense of unfulfillment and alienation leads to a void in her life closely akin to the agony and the lack of fruitfulness. She puts on the light only to find an empty room, which makes her reaction more poignant.

> Do I think of you
> when I hear a step and put on the light
> to find an empty room? ("Do I think of you" 6-8)

In her "In Absentia" she recalls her past association with the lover and expresses her disappointment because of his absence. The rainy days, which used to evoke sensuality earlier, are now painful for her. And winter, which is a symbol of decadence, has now overtaken her:

> This time I know that you are not near
> As before its six chill hits the air
> My lips are chapped, my hair dry
> And mists hide the mornings from eyes that pry. . . .
> I know that winter is here to stay. (7-10, 18)

Like a schizophrenic she has no glee and delight in her life. The parting with the lover seems to her so shocking that even reunion could bring them "no joy." The reality of the present misery becomes too cruel for her to be lived again.

> And from our present misery
> Do yearn to believe
> That that too was a reality
> To be lived again. ("In Absentia" 25-28)

In her distress she further says:

Teeth clenched
Breath held
I wait for your coming
For, from that moment
I must start to live
The coming of your departure. ("In Absentia" 31-36)

Eunice de Souza while discussing her poetry says:

> There is a great deal about blood and sweat and clenched teeth, and about lashing and throbbing, the final effect for the reader is not that of intensity but of embarrassment. The lady doth lash too much. (de Souza 86)

In an interview, Dr. Sandeep Goyal, M.D., Psychiatry, states that delusion of infidelity in which a person thinks that the spouse is cheating him or her is one of the common symptoms of schizophrenia. The same can be seen in Gauri Deshpande's poetry. She doesn't trust her lover's affection, which seems to her:

beyond confines
of need and desire. ("Poems on a Lost Love" 35-36)

She is unable to study his mind:

and have thrilled shivering to think
of what you think
alone in your sleep. (*Ibid.* 37-39)

Despite such a fear the consummation takes place. Even when the act is done, she hesitates to withdraw and continues in that state for some time. Clinically this is called the problem of mutism, one of the features of schizophrenia, in which a person remains silent and doesn't talk to anybody. In one of her poems she complains of her lover's relationship with another woman, and at the same time she knows how to express hatred:

When you divided your love thus—
With your strong and calloused hand
To me fell the harsh. . . .
You chose well, my love
For before you they have been all,

Taught me carefully to read contempt ("When You Divided" 1-10)

Her love poetry is a commentary on male indifference, callousness, insensitivity and exploitation of the female. Cracking under the pressures of chaotic world in which male cruelty and exploitation go hand in hand, she feels torn by the pain and meaninglessness of existence:

And so meaningless is the drift of years
That the only residue is this habit of pain. ("Souvenir" 7-8)

She experiences the all-pervasive pain that comes through body, flesh, heart and spirit. The poetry of Gauri Deshpande is overflowing with "an overwhelming sense of frustration, discontentment, brooding over the past love and an unsuccessful waiting. The lady doth weep too much. . . . There is only one mood—to weep in nostalgia" (Das 61). Monika Varma puts across the same obsession of Gauri Deshpande while talking about her poetry, "Our women poets weep too much in nostalgia" (24). In her frustration, Gauri Deshpande has made death a part of her collective unconscious. She finds a bitter disgusting odour emanating from new-bathed earth in her poem "The Renascence" and in her view:

I wonder why instead of the baked fragrance
The bitter stench arises out of the new-bathed earth.
It is the smell of a death she's hiding in her womb. (1-3)

Like a schizophrenic there is contradiction in speech and thought in the poetry of Gauri Deshpande. "She has not revealed a consistent attitude towards death" (Bajaj 203). In her poem "Death," she says:

you are my friend,
My brother who held my hand at every bend,
My lover about whose neck I must fall now (30-32)

Having declared death to be a Reliever, Lover, Friend and Brother, she expresses a very distinct attitude towards death in her other poems. In "Habit," she says "All dying" and her "living" has become her habit when she "grew up." However, later on in the same poem when she finds death approaching her she presents it as a stranger:

> Now when I see him crossing a street
> to me, coming swiftly
> How am I going to get used to him,
> It's the first time
> And I've had no time (15-19)

She expresses her horror at the mere thought of death in "Kalpavraksha." She wishes for rain and it pours down. The poet says:

> I was frightened thinking
> This fatality of fulfillment
> would lead me into strange
> Lands (6-9)

The similar shocks and frustrations leading to schizophrenic identity are pronounced loudly in Suniti Namjoshi's poetry. However, her frustrations and tensions are mostly the result of her mother's traditional attitude which always hinders her feminist desires. In an interview with Christine Croyden, Namjoshi expresses how her mother disapproves of her freedom:

> She has never been particularly happy that I'm a writer, or, a lesbian feminist. She sees these as notoriety, tarnishing the good name of the family. A section that concerns her is the Fairy Tale. (2)

In the same interview she says, "I belong to India and to the West. Both belong to me and both reject me" (3). She cannot find satisfaction anywhere neither in India nor in the West. She feels like a "Nobody from nowhere." And she doesn't like it. "It is this assertion—this 'means nothing' yet it is there as a fact and cannot be ignored—which Suniti Namjoshi brings into her personal statement" (Varma 5):

> And by upbringing and birth I'm not a citizen
> Of a police state. Not that I hate policemen

And they don't really remind me of anything;
But the policeman said, 'Stop.'
And, my dear, they do exist. ("Various Reasons" 7-11)

This reminds one of the protests made by Hardy in *Tess* and *Jude the Obscure*—that society hinders, man-made institutions restrict the freedom of the individual.

In "Terra and Spectator" a tiny stroke of thought is delightfully concluded by: "And the observer fell asleep on her breast" (5). It is "a little mad—but surely poets must be allowed an extra allowance of lunacy—but it is delicious all the same" (Varma 4). While talking about Suniti Namjoshi's poetry, Monika Varma in her *Facing Four* has used the expression "rueful" again and again. Her writing speaks of her inner dualities, her morbid moods, loneliness and despair:

In the green light of trees,
In the dark light of night,
Past leaves and silver thorns, ("The Unicorn" 2-4)

Her search for identity and self-definition adds to the tensions and conflict in her poetry, taking her women characters to "the verge of schizophrenic existence" (Beniwal 78). In her poem "On Stage," she expresses,

In a wine glass I float,
Whoever I be
And the person who sits talking to them
Is the person They see. (1-4)

Namjoshi's poems are the poems of deep sadness lamenting the lack of pleasure in life. Sometimes she does not seem to be all of a piece because of conflicting emotions. Inner fears, disappointments, frustrations, depressions haunt her.

And she wrote poems because muteness
terrified her,
seeing, as she did, in the level lakewater
an upside down swan. ("And she wrote her poem" 1-4)

The subject matter in contemporary Indian women's poetry has largely shifted from the external world to the psychology of the self. It is the poetry of anxieties and tensions, with greater emphasis on psychological conflict, hate, maladjustment, wounds, rejection and depression.

When I cry my tears trickle into brine
You never saw me cry.
That was sea-water the wind carried off. ("When I cry" 1-3)

C. Vijayasree asserts: "Namjoshi's poetry reflects a mind that is fragmented and at war with itself and the world around. . . . Poetry is, in fact, the means through which she tries to come to terms with her own dividedness and schizophrenic condition." (49)

In her fiercely honest search for identity she reveals her inner contrasts, emotions, feelings, ironies and extremes. Her poems move rapidly through sentiments, anger, sympathy and tensions. Her passionate quest for love sometimes makes her behave in a bizarre manner:

There's sunshine in the garden.
There are flowers in the hall.
At your gate a lovesick beast
Is breaking down the wall. ("Courtship" 1-4)

Namjoshi deplores "the disappointments, deprivation and anguish faced by women who deeply aspire for more space within the existing social structures" (Goel 180). Her "Red Flower" is one of the most successful attempts to look into the agonizing experience of disillusionment in love. The poet assumes the role of a scientific observer studying the red flower which also symbolizes her "bleeding passion of frustrated love" (Chavan, *Fair* 77):

This thing, which sets up the image
Of a shadow flower in my mind, I hold
Away from me, in my hands and examine. (6-8)

The intensity of disappointment is conveyed powerfully and the poet behaves in a very unusual way when she puts the flower and lover's infidelity side by side:

> In the corpse of love, freshly picked
> And the juice still held in the petals. (4-5)

Like other contemporary Indian women poets, Suniti Namjoshi also articulates her inner predicament and personal perplexities with a great intensity so much so that she even doesn't hesitate to turn traditional fables upside down:

> Beauty loved the ugly beast
> and thinking 'twas a prince she'd wed,
> Waited for his shape to change,
> And found there were two beasts in bed.
> ("Beauty and the Beast" 1-4)

Her poetry gives a disturbed note of her feminine sensibility as she is quite aware of the agonized self and unresolved tensions which she is facing. The efforts of her feminine self for fulfillment end in a spectacle of grotesquery. She surprises and shocks everybody by presenting a hard-bitten attitude towards loneliness in love:

> In love and foul weather.
> Love, will you ride with me?
> But my love stayed behind,
> Far away behind me,
> And I rode the wild unicorn
> Past love and foul weather. ("The Unicorn" 5-10)

Her traumatic frustrations resulting in absurd behaviour can also be seen in her poem "Benefits" in which she at first echoes Sarojini Naidu's "If you call me I will come" (7) but then there arises distortion and the poet adds wryly:

> Together we'll make
> many bastards. (8-9)

The society is deadening for Suniti Namjoshi. And her own more liberated world is also filled with anxieties and dualities. In her poem "Ormuzd and Ahriman," the situation is peculiar as both good and evil try to take possession of human soul:

> Ormuzd and Ahriman,
> Black and white demons,
> fought on my doorstep
> like stags in summer. (1-4)

The horrors and anxieties of life turn the attention of the poet towards death and accidents. Man may strive to create a perfect and orderly world but cannot prevent death. In "Columbia, America" the houses grow in a row, trees are orderly and even squirrels are discreet but even then a "jarring note" is struck with a

> bird in a bad taste
> Lying dead on the street. (8-9)

Suniti Namjoshi knows: "Accidents will happen." (10)

The conditions of the modern world are disconcerting enough to jolt the sensitive psyche of these poets and they take to poetry as a means to react to the world around. Suniti Namjoshi also feels terrified with the society and takes poetry as a means of self-expression.

The same miserable lot and helpless condition of a woman is depicted in the poetry of Lalitha Venkateswaran. She faces a struggle against her own self. The traditional make-up of a conventional woman is a factor which persistently forbids her from breaking away completely from the role of a traditional wife. "Debit" is an expression of her unresolved tension: "I would escape your circle if I could do" (1). According to Cora Kaplan, "what many women want is full of contradictions and confusions still entangled in what patriarchy wants them to be or wants for them" (Qtd. Moi 29). The horrors and anxieties of life result in hysterical overtones and outrageous statements:

> And snared in these the shapeless face

> Of me in leaves, in cigarette smoke,
> And between these window panes. ("Framed" 10-12)

Throughout her life she has looked for true love:

> All my life I looked for one
> Who would be more than my unseen
> Half-pondered out, unfinished self. ("Are You the One?" 1-3)

But the quest has never been quenched. As a result her poems get imbued through and through with the shadows of pessimism, despair, and forlornness. Disillusionment overtakes her mind:

> After many summers, winters, rains,
> For me this spring is full of tears. ("Chitrangada" 18-19)

In "Declarations" there is the agony of the deeply felt shock at the lover's infidelity:

> Now a heavy tree has pushed its roots
> With violence beneath our love. (8-9)

The poem probes the agonizing experience of disappointment in love. Her poetry reveals her rage, grief, inner fears and her sense of betrayal. A sense of panic and insecurity is there, making her sound schizophrenic:

> I grope within my emptiness
> For your attentive present arms. ("Attendance" 7-8)

In her poetry, the first person singular is romantic first in expectation of the shape of things to come, but soon that sweet future becomes the sour present. As a result her poems start presenting the miserable lot and helpless condition of a woman:

> I do not know
> Who is the parasite amongst us two:
> Absorbing vampire me, or contended—smiling you. ("Debit" 7-9)

So, the earlier complacence is given a go by; the poetic self gears up to face the troubled world alone. The unresolved tension between the desire and the spasm brings a sense of alienation in her and her poems become an expression of her fears and frustrations:

> I cut all mooring and allowed
> The current's swell to carry me
> Beyond my fear: beyond also
> The reach of your destroying oars. ("Boating" 10-13)

The poem lets us peep into her sufferings and tortured psyche on the one hand and the paradox and complexity of the female psyche on the other hand. The distress and anguish is so much that the poet starts thinking of death. In her poem "Shanker Raman," she calls death "greyness of dust" that "extinguishes all":

> A fact that pulls tears out of old eyes
> And makes the heart strain in vain (8-9)

Eunice de Souza's poetry also reveals her painful encounter with life. Her poems show the feminist struggle of a brave intelligent woman to maintain herself in a world that is, actually, life-denying. Keki Daruwalla in his article "Confessional Poetry as Social Commentary: A View of Indian Poetry in English by Indian Women Poets" while speaking about Eunice de Souza says: "One is not conscious of the poet suffering from any persecution complexes or hallucinatory fears as one reads her. And yet only a part of the above statement is true." (57)

de Souza's childhood experiences of Goan-Catholic community are contained in disturbing memories of a mess of threatening persons—Miss Louise with her obsessive femininity, puritanical nuns and priests, ignorant aunts, silly giggling Goans, the prolific Pillar and even his silent wife—conspiring to obliterate her independent self. Her lonely voice can be heard in *Fix*, the first collection of her poems:

> My cousin Elena
> is to be married. . . .
> her family history examined
> for T.B. and madness
> her father declared solvent

her eyes examined for squints
her teeth for cavities,
her stools for the possible
non-Brahmin worm. ("Marriages are Made" 1-2, 5-11)

Consequently, the underlying meanings of such poetry disclose an atmosphere of subdued tensions, hidden sexuality, and frustrated emotions. Her poetry is the poetry of loss and self-disgust. In the "Introductions" written by Keith Fernandes in de Souza's *Selected and New Poems*, Fernandes expresses her own attitude towards the poetry of Eunice de Souza "There are poems which speak of failure, isolation, disintegration and loss" (xvi). There is deep sadness in her verse. She has attempted to work out her traumas through her poetry. Sometimes she becomes too cryptic and bitter. Her self-expression gets completely bare, stripped of all gloss and glamour. She is instilled with a belief that she is a "lame duck" when she hears her parents "wanted a boy" (16). She is even ready to crucify her female identity:

I heard it said
my parents wanted a boy.
I've done my best to qualify.
I hid the blood-stains
on my clothes
and let my breasts sag. ("de Souza Prabhu" 15-20)

There is no sign of sentimentality and self-pity. de Souza appears extremely apathetic. Extremes of elated or depressed moods coupled with sense of failure are visible:

Right, now here it comes,
I killed my father when I was three.
I have muddled through several affairs
And always come out badly.
I've learned almost nothing from experience.
("Autobiographical" 1-5)

The poem begins by confessing feelings of guilt for her father's early death, for several disastrous love affairs and for learning nothing from experience. Goan vulgarity and the attitude of the

Goan community towards women arouse alienation, frustration, disillusionment, and deep sadness in her poetry. Her poetry appears to be the poetry of defeats and failures. Her suicidal attempt further confirms her schizophrenic identity.

> Yes, I've tried suicide
> I tidied my clothes but
> left no notes. I was surprised
> to wake up in the morning. (*Ibid.*13-16)

The mind of a woman is always filled with a sense of fear: "A woman's life is constantly bogged down by fear and it is one of the main hindrances to her attempt at self-realization. One of the main reasons why women are oppressed by patriarchy is that it is capable of inducing fear into them." (Jena 12) The same fear resulting in delusions of persecution, which is one of the symptoms of schizophrenia, can also be seen in de Souza's poetry as when she claims:

> I thought the whole world
> was trying to rip me up
> cut me down go through me
> with a razor blade. (*Ibid.*23-26)

A false and irrational belief haunts her that she is being cheated, harassed, poisoned or conspired against. People are plotting to harm her. Her poetry reveals her attempted suicides, her rage, grief, inner fears and her sense of betrayal.

> Keep cats
> if you want to learn to cope with
> the otherness of lovers. ("Advice to Women" 1-3)

Thus, "the central question underlying de Souza's work is not the metaphysical 'what is the meaning of life?' but the question, 'what is to be alive?'" (Fernandes ix). Her persona is that of somewhat negative about herself as well as others:

> It was kill or die
> and you got me anyway:

The blood congeals at lover's touch.
The guts dissolve in shit. ("Forgive Me, Mother" 5-8)

Like Sylvia Plath and Anne Sexton, Eunice de Souza's poetry also becomes confessional many times. Nervous breakdown, nostalgic longings, excessive depression and suicidal tendencies are some of the characteristics of the confessional poetry which also mark the poetry of Eunice de Souza:

In school
I clutched Sister Flora's skirt
and cried for my mother
who taught across the road.
Sister Flora is dead.
The school is still standing.
I am still learning
to cross the road. ("The Road" 15-22)

Her inner anguish makes her negative about herself and her poetry becomes tragic and pessimistic revealing her horrifying experiences from which she says she hasn't learnt anything. Throughout her poems the element of discontentment is pervasive:

I head for the abyss with
Monotonous regularity. ("Autobiographical" 6-7)

Her relationship with her mother is also an exasperating and frustrating one. Utter disgust and traumatic experiences lead to a sense of frustration, making her creative art shocking:

I was never young.
Now, I'm old, alone.
In dreams
I hack you. ("Forgive Me, Mother" 9-12)

An identical feministic predicament can also be perceived in the poetic world of Sunita Jain. Her silence says much more than Das' outbursts. However, sometimes she becomes angry and demanding:

you love me
as leaves grow
on clinging vines—
say it again and again till
feeling is a net of veins
flowing with life. ("I Want You to Say" 2-7)

Her helplessness in an unequal battle with the lawmaker man results in a deep and unrelieved sense of loneliness:

The angler
so patient
expectant
the prey
so curious . . .
he tired
she dead. ("The Angler" 1-5, 13-14)

In a personal interview she has expressed her disappointment as her brother who was two years older to her was always more valued by the family. The same dissatisfaction she faced in her "sasural." Filled with the sense of frustration and loneliness, the poet turns to poetry as the exclusive medium for its cathartic release. Poetry responds to the urgent need of the psyche to come to terms with itself which otherwise threatens to collapse under the complex tensions generated by the peculiar experience like:

Many the days that cried for respite
many nights that would not go to sleep. ("Et tu Brute" 4-5)

Annis Pratt feels that marriage brings atrophy to the life of woman, in which she experiences tension, puzzlement and confusion and is cast out if she expresses her natural desires. The compromises and adjustments are the primary reasons for her dissatisfaction in life. The uneasy pressures of uncertain relationships are never far off:

The door bangs
shut upon wifely tensions
(he leaves for work early)

> I gulp in
> breathfuls of the rested air
> and feel the damage
> inside healing. ("The day is not yet light" 9-15)

She writes about love, or rather, the failure of love or the absence of love with the obsessiveness of a woman who can realize her being fully only through love. The mania with love remains unrequited in her life. The resultant strident sense of disappointment and deprivation marks the central theme. In her "Deep in the Dark" we can see her crying for love in despair:

> My body bruised,
> by your lust teeth marked;
> the unsatiable searing
> of our last love
> will it outlive
> this despair?
> Hold me love, hold me near. (6-12)

Her search for identity on a foreign land becomes another reason of her frustration. She feels alienated and frightened in a U.S. town where she sings "Song of Ruth":

> A mid-winter morn
> in a U.S. town
> so empty, still, dead. . . .
> a desolate unending day
> next.
> Windows shut
> curtains drawn.
> Tuck . . . tuck. . .tuck
> A frightened face appears (1-3, 9-14)

The mid-winter morn in a U.S. town is for her "empty, still, dead" and she finds it a "desolate unending day." Sometimes the poet seeks remedy to meaningless of existence in man's love. Love seems to bring contentment to her. Even happiness and self-fulfillment is sought through this love. She seems to find relief from the agony of existence:

> Feel my music,
> my body pregnant with your body. . . .
> We strung instead
> our own taut strings
> and loved like mingled blood
> inseparably ("Feel My Music" 1-2, 8-11)

For her it is physical relationship with lover that gives her "peace":

> Held between your arm spaces
> dulled with loving, . . .
> In your convoluted
> tight grips, see,
> I have turned, my love
> utterly lovely. ("Held Between Your Arm Spaces" 1-2, 5-8)

However, when this love is not attained, her poetry reaches the stage of sickness and breakdown. Her feminine self becomes unable to escape the awareness of being prisoner of her own loneliness.

A similar experience can also be traced in the poetry of Debjani Chatterjee who experiences that in creating new identities, new metaphors and symbols, new bonds and new meanings, a woman confronts patriarchal hegemony at the level of sensibility and reality. And this results in her divided-self and, hence, neurosis.

> I was that woman at the helm of six hundred million,
> Who longed to be accepted as simply human,
> A real person like others, and not a myth.
> I was the woman, neurotic, torn, disowning my sex.
> ("I Was That Woman" 63-67)

She like other women poets epitomizes the predicament of an Indian woman who doesn't like to be treated as a mere object of enjoyment but as an independent and vivacious individual. Time and again in her poem "I Was That Woman" the feeling of a woman of being used by pawing males and of being exploited is hinted at:

> I was the voluptuous, decorative drudge.
> I was the creature with will power raped. (68-69)

The poet's livelihood abroad "In England, Germany, Disneyland" has made her an alienated being on those foreign lands. This living alone has further added to the poet's dissatisfaction:

> In the world's metropolis
> I mount my escalating destiny.
> The loneliness of city jungles
> Shelters the reluctant immigrant
> Amid skyscraper towers of silence. ("The Question" 5-9)

She tells Sita's story and describes her as a

> Dutiful Daughter, perfect wife,
> devoted mother, best of women,
> role model for all time— ("Your Story, Sita" 34-36)

Her behaviour becomes strange as when she relates "the fire test" of Sita to "the dowry-deaths" of present times and a pervasive gloom and sadness haunt her:

> From the blaze when you lifted scorching eyes
> to the crowd with shuffling feet and bowed heads,
> did you foresee the dowry-deaths of your daughters yet
> endure? (*Ibid* 34-36)

Coming back to India also doesn't provide any joy and happiness. Thus, like a schizophrenic, pleasure and joy have ended in her life:

> Here every slimy ditch aspires to be the Ganges,
> The smelly pickpockets have the impish smile
> Of the immortal butter thief. ("The Question" 34-38)

It is the realization that an individual cannot be his/her natural self that leads to the psychological conflict in the Indian women poets' minds which can metaphorically be described as the schizophrenic experience. Schizophrenics live divided lives and the characteristic is clearly evident in the poetry in which the Indian women poets reflect the conflict between their instincts and reality. While talking about the condition of human beings in the present times Terence Smith in his article "Mapping the Postmodern: Deleuze and Guattari's Social Schizophrenia" says:

> This is a period of schizophrenia. . . . Not so much schizophrenic in any clinical sense . . . but schizophrenia considered as a process; a mapping of the topography of the social, cultural or aesthetic rendered in terms of the topography of the mind, such that the fragmentation and increasing alienation of advance capitalism is understood in terms of a collective psychosis. (Smith)

A study of Indian women's poetry reflects this condition.

Lacan, by bringing Freud and Saussure together, emphasized the feeling of "lack" in female psyche as woman feels deprived of the power to create due to biological and anatomical reasons. He asserts that the unconscious and language are both acquired cultural constructs and no pre-given male or female entities exist, thus, emphasizing what Simone de Beauvoir has already aptly described as "One is not born a woman; one becomes one."

Thus, it is the society which is responsible for a woman's schizophrenic identity, and contemporary women poets have well presented this agony of a woman. These poets want freedom from the sort of the thralldom, and want to assert their individuality as human beings. A woman, however, remains dissatisfied with the existing reality where under the dominant patriarchal ideology she is unable to express her true feelings and sentiments. She is baffled and disgusted by the social roles imposed on her which do not provide her with any self-contentment, and looks for a release from her suffocating circumstances. These women are:

> aliens in their own land, trapped by dependency upon male whims, who try to disentangle themselves from wifely behaviour and motherhood where her own children have become strangers . . . and try to escape from the inexorable enclosure to a new environment where 'maleness' and 'femaleness' no longer undermine the

> development of the human personality . . . this new environment is beyond sexual politics, a new kind of space. (Pratt 68)

Coupled with this desire for autonomy and self-definition is the fear of becoming a victim and treated as a deviant if a woman dares to defy patriarchal strictures. Living within this socially imposed identity she feels alienated, both emotionally and socially. This alienation and resultant unresolved tensions breed doubt and confusion, taking her on "the verge of schizophrenia." As Rashmi Bajaj has aptly put: "The callous society turns sensitive persons into schizophrenics" (268).

Taken as a whole, the works of these women poets do not display a wide range and variety of experience as to be witnessed in their male counterparts, still they have succeeded in voicing in their own tender way the aspirations, hopes, fears, frustrations and disappointments of the feminine world. It is the poetry of "sighs and thighs" (Varma 24) and, hence becomes nerve-breaking or neurotic. "For the artist or the poet the unconscious becomes the ideal kingdom of pleasure, a spa by the sea to which he may retreat at will in service of the ego" (Graziano 51). The poetry of the poets taken for study embodies the agonies of a woman emerging from the state of subjugation and bondage and seeking to establish her identity and the self. As a result, the moods of these poets range from despair and dejection to anger and a bewildered sense of rootlessness and further on, resulting in their schizophrenic tendency.

Works Cited

Bajaj, Rashmi. *Women Indo-Anglian Poets: A Critique*. New Delhi: Asian, 1996.

Beauvoir, Simone de. *The Second Sex*. Trans. H.M. Parshley. New York: Vintage, 1952.

Beniwal, Anup. "Identity, Experience, Aesthetic: Indian Women's Poetry in English." *Occasional Papers*. (March 1999): 71-95.

Chavan, Sunanda P. "Modern Indian English Women Poets: An Overview." *Perspective on Indian Poetry in English*. Ed. M.K. Naik. New Delhi: Abhinav, 1984. 190-207.

______. *The Fair Voice: A Study of Indian Women Poets in English*. New Delhi: Sterling, 1984.

Croyden, Christine. Interview with Suniti Namjoshi. *Hecate's Australian Women's Book Review*. Ed. Brook Barbara. 15 May 2007 <http://www.emsah.uq.edu.au/awsr/recent/8.html>.

Daruwalla, K.N. "Confessional Poetry as Social Commentary: A View of Indian Poetry in English by Indian Women Poets." *Contemporary Indian English Poetry*. Ed. Atma Ram. Calcutta: Writers Workshop, 1989.

Das, Bijay Kumar. *Modern Indian-English Poetry*. Bareilly: Prakash, 1992.

De Souza, Eunice. "Kamala Das, Gauri Deshpande, Mamta Kalia." *Contemporary Indian Poetry in English*. Ed. Saleem Peeradina. Delhi: Macmillan, 1997.

Dwivedi, A.N. ed. *Papers on Indian Writing in English*. 2nd ed. Vol. 1. New Delhi: Atlantic, 2001.

Eagleton, Mary. *Feminist Literary Theory: A Reader*. Oxford: Blackwell, 1996.

Fernandes, Keith. Introduction. *Selected and New Poems*. By Eunice de Souza. Bombay: St. Xavier's, 1994.

Gilbert, Sandra, and Susan Gubar. *The Madwoman in the Attic: The Woman Writer and the Nineteenth-Century Literary Imagination*. London: Yale UP, 1979.

Goel, Savita "Suniti Namjoshi's *Feminist Fables*: A Minor Feminist Classic." *Indian Women Writers: Critical Perspectives*. Ed. Jaydipsinh K. Dodiya. New Delhi: Sarup, 2000. 177-82.

Goyal, Sandeep. Personal Interview. 7 Dec. 2007.

Graziano, Frank. "Poetry Writing Therapy and Schizophrenia: A Poet's Point of View." *Literature and Psychology* 29.1 (1979): 49-59.

Jain, Sunita. Personal Interview. 30 June 2007.

Jena, Seema. *Carving a Pattern out of Chaos*. New Delhi: Asian, 1990.

Kalia, Mamta. Interview with Eunice de Souza. *Talking Poems: Conversations with Poets*. New Delhi: Oxford UP, 1999. 57-66.

Kalia, Mamta. Personal Interview. 23 March 2008.

King, Bruce. *Modern Indian Poetry in English*. Delhi: Oxford UP, 1987.

Lessing, Doris. *Martha-Quest*. London: Virgo Press, 1986.

Moi, Toril. *Sexual/ Textual Politics: Feminist Literary Theory*. 2nd ed. London: Routledge, 1988.

Pratt, Annis. *Archetypal Patterns in Women's Fiction*. Bloomington: Indiana UP, 1981.

Sheshadri, Vijayalakshmi. *The New Woman in Indian-English Women Writers since the 1970s*. Delhi: B.R., 1995.

Smith, Terence. "Mapping the Postmodern: Deleuze and Guattari's Social Schizophrenia." 28 May 2008 <http:// homepages.tesco.net/theatre/tezzaland/webstuff/mapping.html>.

Varma, Monika. *Facing Four: A Critical Opinion on the Poetry of Suniti Namjoshi, Gauri Deshpande, Kamala Das, Bharati Sarabhai*. Calcutta: Writers Workshop, 1973.

Vijayasree, C. *Suniti Namjoshi: The Artful Transgressor*. Jaipur: Rawat, 2001.

From Passivity to Stridency: Tackling the Experience

Freedom is perhaps the prerequisite for human life to flourish. Freedom means to be able to breathe freely, to meet people, to have an openness of experience to do as one likes. But in India a woman is kept in kitchens and parlours, whether in purdah or in luxury she is deprived of freedom. To express her wrath against patriarchy, a woman these days is moving outside cultural and disciplinary boundaries and is defying the traditional role of woman as a dutiful wife, mother or daughter. She is trying to break the walls of silence that habitually surround her. But the social pressures which mould her very thinking make her non-communicative about her real needs and desires. As a result there arises a contradiction in speech and behaviour making her sometimes submissive and sometimes harsh. The same is the case with contemporary Indian women poets taken up for study in this project.

The earlier generation of Indian women who were writing sentimental and romantic poetry in the nineteenth and early twentieth century tried to arouse the consciousness of a woman about her duty towards the honour of her family and obedience to the men in her family. Their women protagonists were the embodiment of domestic virtue. The general image of their women characters was like the one presented and projected by the contemporary women poets who exhibit strange behaviour and confused speech which results from the dilemmas faced by women in their daily existence.

Laing argues that the strange behaviour and seemingly confused speech of people undergoing a psychotic stress were ultimately understandable as an attempt to communicate worries and concerns, often in situations where this was not possible or not permitted. Laing stresses the role of society, and particularly the family, in the development of schizophrenia. He argues that individuals can often be put in impossible situations, where they are unable to conform to the conflicting expectations of their peers, leading to a 'lose-lose situation' and immense mental distress for the individuals concerned. In 1956, in Palo Alto, Gregory Bateson and his colleagues Paul Watzlawick, Donald Jackson, and Jay Haley articulated a related theory of schizophrenia as stemming from *double bind* situations where a person receives different or contradictory messages.

The perceived symptoms of schizophrenia are therefore an expression of distress. And the schizophrenic experiences of the contemporary Indian women poets are also an outcome of their tensions. The poets have used different methods to tackle the passivity imposed on them and the ensuing stridency in their tones and behaviour. While Mamta Kalia has taken up irony, ordinariness and confessional mode in her poetry, Gauri Deshpande has written poems frankly discussing love and sexuality. Suniti Namjoshi has used a number of allusions to express her anger and resentment against the patriarchal society which demands mute acceptance from a woman. Lalitha Venkateswaran's poetry is highly intense and personal and Eunice de Souza becomes cryptic and bitter while expressing her annoyance with the traditional Goan-Catholic community. The patriarchal hegemony of English is by no means the only institutional structure within which the feminine self is trapped. Family, workspace, education, economy, self—evidently constitute those binding forces which keep a woman away from exploring the contours of her own "body-language," so to speak.

Mamta Kalia (b. 1940), a bilingual writer, writing both in Hindi and English, has published two volumes of poetry in English—*Tribute to Papa and Other Poems* (1970) and *Poems '1978* (1979). "Her poems deal with frustrations of a woman's life in and outside the house, boredom of married life and chaos of values in society" (Bajaj 19). Forced living in an appalling environment, including her relationship with her father that was all the time a dominating one, her loneliness in a women's hostel just after marriage, her living with a husband who could not differentiate between love and sex, her survival with all those twelve members of the family who are related to her husband, and so on, has made her voice her anger and dissatisfaction with life. By using irony, she concentrates on the ordinariness of women's life and adopts a confessional tone in her attempt to overcome the aggression faced by them in the male-oriented society. She expresses the fear of losing her individuality and identity. She speaks in an ordinary language of an average Indian middle-class woman:

> I cook, I wash,
> I bear, I rear,
> I nag, I wag,
> I sulk, I sag.
> I see worthless movies at reduced rates. . . .
> I put on weight every month. . . .
> and feel happy.
> I am no longer Mamta Kalia. ("Anonymous" 5-9, 14, 17-18)

By using a very ordinary language she delineates the dreary routine of a working woman. Promilla Kapur in her *Marriage and the Working Woman in India* views the female conflict as a corollary of the "ambivalence" in attitude of both the partners towards the woman's employed status:

> The problem is likely to become more acute and accentuated because fulfillment of the two goals for women requires qualities of different types. The attainment of the goal of marriage for a woman in the continuing traditional family structure in India requires self-negation and co-operation, while the achievement of the goal of being a successful, working woman requires self-enhancement and competition. To be successful in marriage the woman has still to be submissive. And the expectation of fulfill-

> ment of these almost contradictory roles and goals was found to be making a working woman most confused and tense. (Qtd. Sheshadri 119)

Mamta Kalia reflects the inner conflicts of a working woman in her poem "They Made Love." The woman finds no enjoyment and pleasure in sex:

> They made love
> And ate sandwiches
> And looked at each other's face—
> Two empty cans. (1-4)

The mechanical and empty attitude of the couple is evident in these lines.

Mamta Kalia pronounces her grins and grudges by using confessional mode. In "Tribute to Papa" she interrogates even her father for his adherence to customs, traditions and sacraments and complains of the generation gap she feels with him. She has fairly liberal views but at the same time she finds it hard to defy the commandments of her father:

> You suspect I am having a love-affair these days,
> But you're too shy to have it confirmed
> What if my tummy starts showing gradually
> And I refuse to have it curetted?
> But I'll be careful, Papa,
> Or I know you'll at once think of suicide. (27-32)

At times she shows her unwillingness to accept all the standards and norms of behaviour and conduct fixed by men. She has a free will and intellect. She is very candid in her poetic expression and confesses whatever she desires in a straightforward manner:

> I want to slap the boy
> who makes love in a café. . . .
> I want to throw away
> all my cosmetics
> I want to reveal
> My real age. ("Compulsions" 5-6, 11-14)

The patriarchal civilization considers woman as a marginalized creature and her destiny is always defined with reference to man. The same society imparts fullest autonomy to a man, instilling pride in him for his manhood and independence. "Social attitudes give courage to men to face difficulties boldly. Passivity is treated as an essential characteristic of femininity, but a boy\man is encouraged to undertake, invent, dare and achieve self-realization" (Gaur 144). In such a society, a woman feels marginalized, cornered, even overwhelmed by the harsh and unpleasant realities of the society. Mamta Kalia while living in such a society confesses her feelings about the vacant and unexciting Sundays. In her anxiety she sometimes yearns for a mate and desires a holiday schedule full of activity:

> I wander at the emptiness
> of this Sunday and of all Sundays.
> It was never like this
> when you were here. . . .
> We'd go places, visit friends, eat *bhel puri,*
> We'd come back, make love again, call it a day.
>
> ("Sunday Song" 22-25, 31-32)

Her poetry is a confessional one as she confesses her feeling and experience, guilt and hate, love and lust. It is self-revelatory, a poetry of private details. For example, in one of her poems she doesn't hesitate to articulate her impatience with the social etiquettes, and makes a frank declaration of her desires for natural life:

> I want to shout in the middle of the road,
> "I have a name; I'm Sheela,
> I've studied four classes in Prathamik Shala,
> Once I went to a picnic and drank Coca-Cola,
> I can roll excellent *chapattis.*" ("Self- Pity" 9-13)

She feels lost and betrayed, unable to trust the life that is offered to her. There is a constant tension and conflict in her mind. Home for her is not a haven of peace, comfort, and solace, but a dangerous and threatening place. In her poems Mamta Kalia confesses the tedium of everyday household chores, which pressurize a woman because she has to cater to the needs of all the members of her family:

> I feel like crying all the time
> Or running on the roads with an unwashed face.
> I want to smash a glass early in the morning
> And wake up everybody with a start.
> ("I Feel Like Crying All the Time" 1-4)

Disgusted with the people around her, she pronounces her boredom in the same poem. Sometimes she becomes bitter and harsh in her tone:

> I hate these people around,
> Related to me. (5-6)

Her cryptic tone is the result of the passivity imposed on her. She confesses very easily that she is weak and is unable to fight the whole society. That's why, she decides to write:

> In my hour of discontent
> I neither shout nor rant
> I simply fill ink in my pen
> And spill it with intent. ("In My Hour of Discontent" 1-4)

Irony is the hallmark of Mamta Kalia's poetry. In a personal interview, when she was asked about choosing irony as a medium of expression, she replied:

> The only way of writing is that you wear some extra nails or extra fangs or tusks only then you can be read. Nowadays people require ampicillin for cold and cough, ginger is no longer effective. The same is the case with language. You have to evolve your own diction and language as you have to work on content.

Irony is considered by most of the contemporary Indian women poets as the only medium by which they can express their feelings and discontentment with the patriarchal society. In the poem

"Sheer Good Luck," she tells ironically and wittily how jaded and lacklustre her wedded life has turned out to be:

> So many things
> could have happened to me (1-2)

But nothing ever happened to her except "two children" and "two miscarriages" (17).

In her "Tribute to Papa," the tribute becomes a pregnant site of generational difference with regard to values, ideals and way of looking at each other and the world around. Mamta Kalia rejects her father's life of "limited dreams" (7). She intends to choose her own course and follow her ideals. Ironically, she terms her father to be "an unsuccessful man" (5) and delineates the clash between the old and new value scales. That's what a "Lower Division Clerk, Accounts Section" can be:

> You want me to be like you, Papa,
> Or like Rani Lakshmibai.
> You're not sure what greatness is,
> But you want me to be great.
> I give two donkey-claps for your greatness
> And three for Rani Lakshmibai. (17-22)

Thus, in this poem she rejects her father's notions of greatness and the Indian model of a woman as Lakshmibai who fought and died in one sense not for the sake of women but for her son—something that patriarchy would not mind. The poem marks the poet's protest against the disappointing lack of values in the younger generation and the resultant communication gap between the old and the young. The poet ironically regrets her father's lack of courage in the lines:

> I wish you had guts, Papa,
> To smuggle eighty thousand watches at a stroke,
> And I'd proudly say, "My father's in import-export
> business, you know."
> I'd be proud of you then. (8-11)

This could also be a desperate attempt to escape the boredom of a monotonous life.

In her second volume of poems, irony becomes a vital means of surviving through the boredom caused by a steady love-relationship of many years following marriage. The monotony and lack of pleasure in life is expressed by exploring the present in terms of the past ironically:

> My hair held a fragrance once—
> A fragrance you associated with so many flowers. . . .
> Now when I lower my head
> You only see dandruff and grey hair.
> ("My Hair Held a Fragrance Once" 1-2, 5-6)

Mamta Kalia's life is quite uneventful as compared to the other women poets taken for study. And to capture the ordinariness of this uneventful life, she has used ordinary language. So much so that to give free expression to her feelings and emotions she, like most of the other contemporary women poets, has not paid much attention to the formal part of style. In her "In Delhi," she emerges as a critique of society and expresses the dryness of life lived by people in metro cities. The poem is just a "capsule" (Bajaj 310) verse:

> In Delhi
> the sea
> could have really gone dry! (1-3)

Women in India have always remained suppressed and oppressed and this has led to confusion in the mind of an Indian woman so much so that she wants to give proof for everything that she says. She is uncertain whether the people surrounding her believe her or not. The same insecurity is revealed in the style of Mamta Kalia's poetry. Her constant use of parenthesis is a revelation of this. In her poem "Love Made a Housewife out of Me" she says:

> Love made a housewife out of me.
> I came with a degree in Textile Designing,

Skill in debates, dramatics and games
(You can see my certificates.) (1-4)

Sacrifice, submissiveness, excessive endurance and self-effacement are continuously demanded from a woman. As a result, she undergoes a struggle to retrieve her subjugated position and suffers conflicts and traumas in the process. All this has affected the poetry of women poets, too. In their ordinariness these poets question each and everything in the society. The method as a result becomes interrogative:

Who cares for you, papa?
Who cares for your clean thoughts, clean words, clean teeth?
Who wants to be an angel like you?
Who wants it? ("Tribute to Papa" 1-4)

There is nothing in her life but the "prosaic details" of "pending phone calls," "dirty linen," "a shaky mountains of books," "a much needed hair wash" (Kalia, *Interview with Eunice de Souza* 65). The relative ease with her medium and down-to-earth realism with which she captures her mundane, middle-class existence has helped initiate what Bruce King terms as "the present contemporary manner" (155). Virginia Woolf's *A Room of One's Own* also expresses the ironical paradox of a woman's life. According to her, a woman is of the highest importance imaginatively; however, she is completely insignificant practically.

Gauri Deshpande (b. 1942) is another poet who has earned a niche for herself. Her poetic corpus includes three volumes—*Between Births* (1968), *Lost Love* (1970) and *Beyond the Slaughter House* (1972). Her love poetry is different from the love poetry of other Indian poets; she has rejuvenated the tradition of love poetry by a contemporary new voice. There is reconsideration and reassessment of the experience of love. Though love is considered as giving eternal pleasure in some of her poems, she seems to be quite aware of the dreams which shatter because of love:

Slightly unwelcome, taciturn, you moved in

and we lived on in disharmony,
slowly, silently the green came into trees,
your harsh eyes ate into the decay of my dreams
and the sound of your night pacing grew in my bloodstream. (3-7)

At the same time love seems to give her endless contentment. In "There Was a Time" love gives her "abundant recompense" for a loveless past and an uncertain future. It has more than made up for the times when they were not together:

And our solace
Will be: we knew
Of you and me. (18-20)

Even the memories of love have their own significance. For Gauri Deshpande the dearest treasure is an old letter with violets preserved in its leaves and she feels that memories are essential "otherwise there's nothing." The very intensity of her love sometimes becomes painful because it involves almost slavish attachment:

And attached by the same
Painful devotion and self-loss
To the feet of God
I'd be canonized ("December" 7-10)

Here she doesn't seem to be much different from the early Romantics like Toru Dutt and Sarojini Naidu. However, it is her frank, free and uninhibited portrayal of sex that makes her different from these early poets. In order to flout the rules which patriarchy has set up as norms, women poets like Gauri Deshpande have unreservedly expressed their sexual desires and have, thus, replaced the earlier timidity and tenderness. In fact, free expression of sexuality is an act of self-assertion and freedom according to the feminist point of view. *Lost Love* reveals Gauri Deshpande's concept of love as modified by her attitude to sex because "What was in *Between Births* an innocent flower of love has become in this volume a blood-stained symbol of sexorgy. Sex is now almost a substitute for love" (Saha 44). In "Poems on

Lost Love" she uses the imagery of earth and rain to suggest the act of consummation:

> I am earth.
> Vast deep and black
> and I receive
> the first rain
> sweet, generous
> lashing, throbbing; . . .
> Yellow daisies burst out
> on my breast and thigh
> at its very touch. (19-24, 28-30)

For her sex is a natural desire and an irresistible biological need. It gives her delight and pleasure. Even while revelling in the physical act, Gauri Deshpande expresses her contempt and distaste for sexual pleasure which reveals her bafflement in this patriarchal world. She finds modern love-making devoid of intensity as men do not plunge into

> the plunging depths of our souls
> and bodies. ("No More" 4-5)

Her nights are spent in "causeless researching" (8) and waking in the mornings is "dull, flat and/ unprofitable" (16-17). She considers the final outcome of this physical act as moving into the "darkness" from the "good fortune" of smiles and caresses. The act is itself a mere ritual:

> Even the ragged breath may be due merely to overweight
> Mental calculator says only five more minutes ("Ritual" 9-10)

She doesn't desire her lover to be physically present with her as his closeness makes her feel disgusted with "bareness of your presence." There is disillusionment and disappointment with love. She finds love-making most unsatisfying. While going through her poems H.L. Amga observes: "Her conceptual strategies seem to hover between two extremities of love, the one dealing with the exuberant feeling of conjugal satiety, and the other with the etiolate nausea or boredom, which comes after the surfeit of love." (186)

She shows woman as dismayed by the non-fulfillment of physical as well as emotional cravings:

When you divided our love thus—
With your strong and calloused hand
To me fell the harsh
Waking up of cold nights
The tired soothing, the quiet
Retreat and unquestioning emptiness
The illness and magnifying of flaws.
You chose well, my love ("When You Divided" 1-8)

Her treatment of love and sexuality shows how much she is dissatisfied with the society which demands silent acceptance from a woman. Though the poet doesn't become strident like Mamta Kalia and Eunice de Souza who adopt an aggressive tone, yet she is quite aware of the "gnawing unrest" of her life that gives her pain and suffering. She longs for a haven of peace:

I'm affected by a prowling unrest
And know not what to do
With my fists that clench and unclench
Thoughts come pouring in my eyes
And drain away leaving a whorl of dirt.
If only it'd rain
If only I'd die. ("Integration" 1-7)

Sometimes the harshness which is a major feature of contemporary poetry written by women is also found in her poetry. "Portrait" is a poem written with a caustic pen. It cleverly brings forward the juxtaposition of the conventional Christmas day—its mother and child—against "dug wrinkled hanging papless down/ Depending from it a bundle" (3-4)—the Madonna and the Dame of the Streets.

A woman feels marginalized, cornered, even overwhelmed by the harsh and unpleasant realities of the society. She demands some space in such a situation:

Oh let me go out into the rain. . . .
Then like a lizard I'll lie
Between sliding mud and water, . . .
And feel my limbs from time to time
As they send down roots and sprout shoots.
("Oh Let Me . . ." 1, 5-6, 9-10)

She like any other new woman has emerged with her own desires, ambitions and quests to break away the shackles of age-old customs, beliefs and mores. But the attempt to fight against the repressive forces of tradition and prescriptive roles based on idealized modes of a bygone era and her desire of newer, wider horizons only results in her living a dual existence; feel confused, angry and reactive. The style of her poetry is an exposure of all this.

The short-line poems of Gauri Deshpande reveal her "useless mournings" for her lost love. She has varied the line-length within her poems as this mode gives her greater freedom to express the mood and feel of the moment. It gives her the opportunity to express the natural flow of poetic frenzy without being unduly worried about the binding rod of syllabic number:

Without wondering how, when, why, or where
We live and meet with death
Turning a street corner.
But I want to see him coming
Scan his face joyously. ("Death" 1-5)

Repetitions within a line like "The sun poured and poured" (Sun 1) and at the beginning of successive lines can be seen in her poetry:

If only it'd rain
If only I'd die
If only there were someone to fall in love with.
If only the day was all done with ("Integration" 6-9)

Such repetitions intensify her feelings for her lost love. Thus, while her love poems voice her emotions and experiences, they also reflect a constant dilemma and conflict in the backdrop.

Suniti Namjoshi (b.1941) is another poet gifted with ironic perception and wit. Her poetic volumes in English are *Poems* (1967), *More Poems* (1971), *Cyclone in Pakistan* (1971), *The Jackass and the Lady* (1980), *The Authentic Lie* (1982), *Flesh and Paper* (1986) and *Because of India: Selected Poems and Fables* (1989). Her "deep sense of horror and disgust in the matters of love and sex" (Dwivedi 208) has taken her towards lesbianism. Presently she is living in Devon, England, with her partner, the poet and the writer, Gillian Hanscombe. She is a Research Fellow at the Centre for Women's Studies at Exeter University. Because of her education from a boarding school, she is connected more with Christianity than Hinduism.

On the one hand, Suniti Namjoshi draws on the Christian ethos with its chapels and sanctuaries and on Adam and Cain, on the other, by her reference to Glaucus, the sea-god, she evokes the world of Greek mythology. She also draws on the Ganges and the "princes" and the gods of the Orient. By deconstructing the allusions, she "tries to combat women's feelings of isolation and inadequacy" (Goel 180).

While talking about Namjoshi's poetry, Jasbir Jain says "Poetry is a friend as well as a skeleton—the warmth and the coldness permeate together and under the subterfuge of warmth and health it is leading the poet slowly towards destruction" (111). In order to express her strong sense of discontentment with the values prevalent in the society, she is even deconstructing the allusions in her poems.

Her poem "Cain" draws upon the Christian allusion and tells about the erratic going on in the mind of the poet. The poem is a deconstructive reading of an old myth. Cain and Abel do not symbolize the binaries of evil and good as the mythical text suggests, but are "Two souls lodged in one body" (3). The poem is a monologue addressed to Abel who symbolizes the "variation of the self" and through withdrawal, invites destruction:

> Listen, my brother, variation of self,
> I respect the battles of schizophrenic.
> Two souls lodged in one body,
> We could split the hemispheres,
> Your share, my share the less. (1-5)

Any rigid separation of these two souls and two worlds is sophistry. The surgeon's knife separates these two worlds and perhaps in doing this destroys them:

> You have fixed a door
> To your room that you might be
> Undisturbed in your little kingdom.
> Two worlds: unshared, unnatural.
> I come to you with the surgeon's knife. (9-13)

Suniti Namjoshi prefers schizophrenic battles within the divided self to such sophistry.

In her poem "The Death of an Old Adam" she uses mythical reference to describe death and considers life as a wish and a hope. She has made Adam a symbol of death which is the reversal of the myth of Eve. In Christianity it is Eve who is accountable for Adam's downfall—for she is the one who persuades Adam to eat the forbidden fruit. Tertullian (known as "Father of the Latin Church") said to his female followers: "You are the devil's gateway" ("Oppression" 1). However, Suniti Namjoshi's poem presents the idea that Adam, the first man, is responsible for bringing death into the world. She shows how one strives and struggles in life despite knowing that death is an unavoidable fact:

> "I have lived a long time.
> "I have lived a short time
> "And circled round the fields. . . .
> "What I ventured, what I wanted, what I won,
> "I had to be me, whatever I did. (6-8, 11-12)

However, the paradox occurs when the poet says that the events in life are inevitable and are finally rounded off by death. She probes the inevitability of this final termination with rare courage:

> Now dirt is dead and hurt is dead.
> Not getting is dead.
> There's nothing to get. (13-15)

Death as a predator—flying over the dead man's eyes—is later on echoed in relation to the sense of smell:

> But the fields will be empty and who
> Will smell the damp earth in his nostrils. (18-19)

"The Unicorn" also comments on the dualities in the poet's mind. The poet rides the wild unicorn while the lover stays behind. Soon the poet enters the world which is lonely and wild and yet enchanting enough. The image of the unicorn in the poem "evokes all that is strange and mythical" (Jain 114). The unicorn becomes a symbol of the unknown and the imaginary and represents a world at once desirable and unattainable. It gives her a handle to demolish the patriarchal notions of female chastity:

> I rode the wild unicorn, . . .
> Past leaves and silver thorn,
> In love and foul weather.
> Love, will you ride with me?
> But my love stayed behind,
> Far away behind me. (1, 4-7)

In "Bed Time Story" a paramour kills a lover giant with the lady's help and climbs into bed. In her "Benefits" a modern lover has many benefits to offer to his lady love. He will bring for her red cheeked apples pre-packed in Eden and "crush-proof" clothes. This new Prometheus will bring flame in a "little jewel box" to put the lady on fire:

> For your pleasure I'll be the new Prometheus

bringing you fire in a little steel box,
a little jewel-box with a flame to be kindled. (4-6)

And then comes the anticlimax and she says: "Together we'll make/ many bastards" (8-9).

Her aversion towards love and sex with a male turns her satire into an utterly nauseating and repulsive one. The famous legend, *Beauty and the Beast*, comes under her nasty satire and scorn. The poem is a deconstructive reading of an old tale as in the end "there were two beasts in the bed" (4).

A woman in the society is considered as an appendage who believes in passive acceptance of whatever is accorded to her. She is not permitted to go beyond the canon of authenticity as this means the defiance of social norms of ideal womanhood. All this has given a bitter tone to Suniti Namjoshi. Her abhorrence with the sexual act has given "a dry, ironic, and cynical tone" (Iyengar 684) to her poems:

in the end. We mated
like dogs. ("Metamorphoses" 17-18)

She has even given new meanings and possibilities to the image of Pinocchio, the long nosed hero of the nursery tales. It is a very powerful poem as it reveals the desire of the poet to remain in illusions as the truth will be unbearable. She is apprehensive that she might smudge the miracle with her fingertips:

That you are made of ivory and steel
And very beautiful, and I'm afraid
To smudge the miracle with my fingertips? ("Pinocchio" 4-6)

She considers it safe to conceal the desire under a powdered mask rather than confront it. It is better if Pinocchio remains a ghost, a dream or a doll "Oh, be a ghost/ In the moonlight, be a dream" (11-12). But this illusion of innocence is sure to be shattered sometimes and it would then be imperative for her and Pinocchio:

We're neither wood nor ivory, they'd switch on

The lights and the children would scream
And we would have to move
To the other side of the curtain. (23-26)

The Christian parable of prodigal son receives a new significance in the modern context in:

So He gives me eternal life.
Profligate, I, say, "Here's a pickle,
How shall I spend eternity?" ("Parable" 6-8)

She writes that she chooses to depict herself as a "bird, beast and fish" (Namjoshi 35) to express the complete otherness, the alienation of woman in patriarchal world. She has none of the "stupid sexual modesty" (Cixous 543) about the body which so enrages Cixous (years of patriarchy have taught women to be ashamed of their bodies and their own desires if that body and those desires are independent of male satisfaction).

Moreover, while employing these allusions, Suniti Namjoshi has forgotten most of the bindings of style. Like Mamta Kalia she has shown fascination for "capsule verse":

In a wine glass I float,
Whoever I be,
And the person who sits talking to them,
Is the person They see. ("On Stage" 1-4)

In her frank expression, she has overlooked the earlier usual pattern of all left-hand capitalization. Even she has not hesitated in introducing mid-line or mid-verse capitalization of letters and sentences. Her poem "After Ionesco" concludes:

NO BODY COMMUNICATES ANYMORE
Here,
        Here is
                My vouchsafe.
Please,
        Please,
                DON'T CRY. (32-38)

On one hand, society wants a woman to conform to the tradition-bound concepts of womanhood chained to the prevailing traditions and customs. On the other hand, she is impelled by an urge to seek a new and just way of life. The result is the confused speech which is prevalent in the poetry of contemporary Indian women poets. Suniti Namjoshi's mid-line and mid-verse capitalization of letters and sentences is also reflective of such perplexed behaviour. The repetition within a line further intensifies the poet's feeling of confusion:

> What I ventured, what I wanted, what I won,
>
> ("The Death of Old Adam" 11)

Her interrogative method like Mamta Kalia's gives the feeling of infinity and uncertainty which hovers in the mind of the poet because of the inner conflicts which a woman has to face in a patriarchal society. In "Unicorn" she is unsure whether her lover would accompany her in "foul weather." She asks, "Love, will you ride with me?" (6) In "The Head of the Roses" she asks herself:

> Was it courage or fear that kept us silent
> Watching the dragonfly over the water? (10-11)

Thus, Suniti Namjoshi is a poet with "variety of subjects and ranges" (Vijayasree 13). Her works are rich in allusions. She draws on Greek or Christian myths and legends, fables and fairy tales, old and new writers and weaves an intricate network. She seems to be extremely perturbed by the painful surroundings that have made her so cynical and skeptical. Her inner self is disconcerted and conflict-ridden. By turning the allusions and legends upside down, she strives to resolve her inner conflicts.

Lalitha Venkateswaran whose poetic career includes three volumes viz. *Declarations* (1970), *Rocking Horse* (1973) and *Tree Bird* (1975) faces a struggle against her own self. She adopts a different method of stridency which is the result of the general attitude towards a woman. She covets softness and tenderness of love: "That was the hour I treasure most" ("Bubbles" 10) and brings out the effect of the transforming power of love:

> Your love gives beauty back to me.
> With you I am invincible. ("Fired" 1-2)

She becomes caring and concerned for other people:

> No matter if you care or not
> For this I give, I care, I care. ("Its Shape" 8-9)

Love and passions are quintessential to her existence. Her poems bear the weight of her intense passionate feelings, so much so that she cannot put up with the shattering of desires and the loss of love:

> And now, without much wanting to,
> I find myself caught too with you;
> And dare not cut through, lest I find
> The fictions of your netted mind. ("Fictions" 5-8)

Her poetry is an expression of the changing attitude of the society towards love. On one hand, she is beaming with love and laughter, beauty and delight in the company of her lover:

> My body learns a new delight
> In its sweet curves and in the shape
> Of fitting to your need and you.
> I want no mirror now to speak,
> Since all reflection's naught with you. ("Fired" 3-7)

On the other hand, her poetry marks a definite break away from the traditional practice of the 19th century poets with regard to the treatment of love. She doesn't treat it as something idealistic, divine, or idyllic, but as a hard physical reality and as an inevitable biological necessity. She pines for love but she cannot compromise like an average woman with any imposed situation. She is conscious of her identity and feminine grace:

> My memories are the heart of me,
> My laughter is the start of me;
> My selfish tears a part of me. ("I Do Not Wish" 5-7)

She freely expresses the desire for a male body. In "Inventory" she dotingly details the face that haunts her—his low shining cap of hair, tender brown eyes, flat clean jaw and miraculous neck:

> I would commit your face to memory:
> Your eye-low shining cap of hair
> And your white gash
> Of face; slant-lashed, tender, . . .
> Unsheathed delight in nakedness.
> You. A continual feature in my thoughts. (1-4, 14-15)

She expresses her pleasure in physical act with all its intensity. Her body in "Fired" learns "new delight" (3) in the shape of "fitting to" his "need" (5). She hangs her "coat of passion" on his "pointed breast." However, she expresses her denigration and scorn against this physical love with same intensity. She protests against the merely physical in love. In her "Declaration" she asks her lover, "Why must you always have it so?" (10) Her contempt bursts forth:

> There has not been a day
> which was not seeded thus. (6-7)

She expresses her desire to "escape/ The mesmerism" ("Debit" 2-3) of the lover's body.

The method of this new poet is largely interrogative. She questions the whole patriarchal society with all her intensity. Her "Declaration" is one of its own kinds as the entire poem is made up of questions only. Most of her poems end with a question which she poses to the society in her anxiety:

> What could I say?
> Could there be
> A somewhat better form for me
> Of public truthfulness? ("Public" 15-18)

In a society which pressurizes a woman to undergo silent suffering, she cannot openly express herself, and if she tries to articulate she remains unsure whether the society is paying any heed to her words. This bewildered existence results in a tendency to repeat whatever she wants to communicate. In her eagerness to express her desire of not sharing herself, she repeats the same line at the end of the poem:

> I do not wish to share myself
> With you or others, friend and foe. . . .
> For I do not wish to share myself. ("I Do Not Wish" 1-2, 9)

In the same poem she repeats the words "of me" at the end of three successive lines. In order to intensify the meaning and to give vent to her feelings more forcefully. Lalitha Venkateswaran has used this unique method of starting and ending a poem with similar set of lines. Her poems "Debit" and "Chitrangada" reflect this trait:

> For me this spring is full of tears.
> Until I met you, . . .
> For me this spring is full of tears. (Chitrangada 1-2, 19)

Eunice de Souza (b.1940) writes extensively on Indian culture and literature. Her verse collections are *Fix* (1979), *Women in Dutch Painting* (1988), *Ways of Belongingness* (1990) and *Selected and New Poems* (1994). Her memories of Goan Catholic life in Poona represent the repressions, prejudices, ignorance, social injustice and the place of women in that society. Disappointed with the patriarchal hegemony, she becomes comparatively more bitter and harsh in her tone as compared to other contemporary poets. Her use of irony is more bitter than Mamta Kalia.

> Mamta Kalia's irony often becomes a mere substitute for her anger and disgust signifying nothing. . . . Irony becomes far more meaningful in the poetry of Eunice de Souza than that of Mamta Kalia because it is the exclusive means through which she can come to terms with her Goan-Catholic identity. (Chavan 200)

Eunice de Souza expresses her resentment against the Goan-Catholic society in such a way that it makes her tone strident. Many of her poems are the revelation of this harsh attitude:

No matter that
my name is Greek
my surname Portuguese
my language alien.
There are ways
of belonging.
I belong with the lame ducks. ("de Souza Prabhu" 8-14)

She is bitterly satirical in attacking the stereotyped treatment of feminine experience by poets in her poem "Poem for a Poet." In "My Students" she says:

My students think it funny
that Daruwallas and de Souzas
should write poetry.
Poetry is faery land forlorn.
Women writers Miss Austen.
Only foreign men air their crotches. (1-6)

"The engines of her rage are fuelled by the language that is as it was fissioned for destructive effect" (Iyengar 728). She presents a satirical picture of a Casanova in her poem "He Speaks." The whole physical act is reduced to mere mockery as the philanderer finds her act as "pathological display" and decides to "fix her." Next time after the physical act, he tells her very casually:

I hope you realize I do this
With other women. (33-34)

While writing about her poetry, K.R Srinivasa Iyengar says "Has she dipped her pen in acid? Is Eunice amusing herself throwing spoonful of boiling oil on fellow Goans, fellow Catholics, fellow humans?" (Iyengar 727) In her poem "Autobiographical," her lines capture the hostility of words as when she speaks of "the whole world" (23) which is "trying" (24) to "go through" (25) her "with a razor blade" (26). She further says:

then I discovered
a cliché: that's what I wanted
to do to the world. (27-29)

Her scathing attack on the way in which matrimonial alliances are made can be seen in her "Marriages are Made." The whole institution of marriage is scorned in this poem. She satirizes the pettiness of the society. She has mentioned the allusion "Marriages are Made" in heaven ironically. Cousin Elena is examined for her family history, the solvency of her father, her height, health and colour before the other family decides she will do "justice" to their "good son of Mother Church":

> She's not quite tall enough
> and not quite full enough
> (children will take care of that)
> Her complexion it was decided
> would compensate, being just about
> the right shade
> of rightness
> to do justice to
> Francisco X. Noronha Prabhu
> good son of Mother Church. (12-21)

Francis X D' Souza, "father of the Year" ("Catholic Mother" 1), has seven children in seven years and declares "We're One Big Happy Family" (8) and there is his silent, suffering and always pregnant wife:

> the pillar's wife
> says nothing. (17-18)

Eunice de Souza has taken the place of a woman capable of resenting and rebelling against this "status" of an ideal woman conforming to the *Pativrata* code. Sometimes her personal grouses and frustrations overpower her so much that she "becomes waspish and combative, and loses control over her diction" (Singh 94). In one of her poems, she says:

> Mamas never mentioned menses.
> A nun screamed: You vulgar girl
> don't say brassieres
> say bracelets. ("Sweet Sixteen" 3-6)

In India a girl is an unwanted being. She is a victim of indifference. Most couples prefer male children because of the feeling that the boys will carry on the family name. According to Manu, "A man conquers the world by the birth of a son: he enjoys eternity by birth of a grandson; and the great grandfather enjoys eternal happiness by the birth of a grandson's son" (Qtd. Gupta 44). Eunice de Souza has also remained a victim of this indifference. She claims that she belongs with "the lame ducks" ever since she heard her parents "wanted a boy" (16). Sandra Lee Bartky's "On Psychological Oppression" analyses how the woman inherently develops an inferiority complex. According to her, "women can be oppressed in ways that need involve neither physical deprivation, legal inequality, nor economic exploitation." She is a "victim of psychic alienation or psychological oppression. . . . The psychologically oppressed become to themselves their own oppressors; they come to exercise harsh dominion over their own self-esteem" (34). The same is presented in the poetry of Eunice de Souza. She too had fallen into the trench of identity crisis:

> I heard it said
> my parents wanted a boy.
> I've done my best to qualify.
> I hid the blood-stains
> on my clothes
> and let my breasts sag. ("de Souza Prabhu" 15-22)

These futile efforts of holding back her feminine feelings and trying to prove herself a boy make her tone harsh and sardonic so much so that her own community denounces her as "betrayer" (de Souza 38). Her *Fix* has been denounced as a "hard-edged and violent book" (23) by R.S. Pathak. The book was denounced from the pulpit at St. Peter's in Bandra, and Adil Jussawalla said that if she continued in the same vein, she would soon be denounced at St. Peter's in Rome. She even rebels against her family upbringing. Some of her poems show her conflict with her parents. In one of her poems, while addressing her mother she says:

> Forgive me, mother,
> that I left you
> a life-long widow
> old, alone. . . .
> In dreams
> I hack you ("Forgive Me, Mother" 1-4, 11-12)

Many of her poems are a revelation of her existential dilemma. In her desire to move from bondage to freedom, from indecision to self-assertion, and from weakness to strength, at times her poetry becomes a tale of lacerated psyche and at such times she yearns for peace and tranquillity:

> God rock. I'm a pilgrim.
> Tell me—
> Where does the heart find rest? ("Pilgrim" 11-13)

The poem also reveals the poet's use of the interrogative method like other women poets. Her dwindling between self-isolation and self-assertion results in a bafflement which can be seen in her repetition of lines:

> the limbs keep flopping
> the sawdust keeps popping
> out of the gaps
> out of the gaps
> out of the gaps
> sister ("Eunice" 10-15)

The poet has used capitalization when it is required by usage, without any automatic capitalization of all left-hand margins. Sometimes she introduces new sense and sentence with capital letters:

> Keep cats
> if you want to learn to cope with
> the otherness of lovers.
> Otherness is not always neglect—

Cats return to their litter trays
when they need to. ("Advice to Women" 1-6)

The poetry presents the image of a suffering woman preoccupied with her inner world, and her predicament in a male-dominated society. Sometimes in her bewilderment, she uses parenthesis to express whatever she finds difficult to express otherwise:

There's a sun in the sky
and you are near me
and all should be right with the world.
But something hasn't set
(and it had better not be the sun!) ("Unfinished Poem" 2-6)

The poet's confessional mode here reveals the insecurity of her mind. Though in her later poems she seems to be yearning for peace and comfort at the cost of her inner and suppressed desires, yet there is a constant undercurrent of frustration and tension.

Thus, many of her poems are satires or are written in a confessional mode "similar to Sylvia Plath's miming of deep fears and resentments which are expressed through self-ironic wit" (King 156). The subjects of her satire and stridency are the church, marriage, Catholic motherhood, Indian colour prejudice, sexual prudery and hypocrisy, Goan vulgarity and the alienation felt by many Goan Catholics towards Hindu India. Adil Jussawalla aptly points out: "Those readers who prefer a softer or more lyrical line around its edge may find it extremely unpleasant" (90).

In order to tackle the male supremacy, the new poets oscillate between regression and full vigilance which results in a creative product. Maire Jannus Kurrik in a critical essay writes: "We uphold the creation of art as something created by the whole psyche, by the conscious and the unconscious. We accept that a temporary regression from the world of rational consciousness may be a necessary moment in poetic creation, but we stress conscious ego control." (Qtd. Graziano 50)

To defy the notions of patriarchy, a woman speaks with many tongues. Sometimes, she speaks illogically in fits and starts. Shormistha Panja writes: "And it is these pulsations that express a oneness with one's own body and with the world outside the body that Lacan maintains disappears after the child moves from the imaginary to the symbolic order with the learning of language and of difference." (96)

Thus, the contemporary poets have learnt the new alphabet of their body and speak in non-habitual ways in starts, pauses, and ellipses. At times they use parenthesis and even break the syntax. The preference is always for irony and ordinariness. Tones are deliberately flat and unpoetic. Their expressions of love and sexuality are also sometimes passive and sometimes bitter. At times the poets are using a number of allusions which also illustrate their advance towards stridency. Their poetry is highly intense and personal. Woman's language is different from a man's language as it lies in the "no man's land, the spaces between alphabets" (Panja 97). However, everything expressed by these women poets whether the tone is passive or harsh shows their resentment against male-dominated society.

Works Cited

Amga, H.L. *Indo-English Poetry*. Jaipur: Surabhi, 2000.

Bajaj, Rashmi. *Women Indo-Anglian Poets: A Critique*. New Delhi: Asian, 1996.

Bartky, Sandra Lee. "On Psychological Oppression." *Philosophy and Women*. Ed. Sharon Bishop and Marjorie Weinzweig. California: Wordsworth, 1979. 33-41.

Chavan, Sunanda P. "Modern Indian English Women Poets: An Overview." *Perspective on Indian Poetry in English*. Ed. M.K. Naik. New Delhi: Abhinav, 1984. 190-207.

Cixous, Helene. "Laugh of the Medusa." *The Theory of Criticism: From Plato to the Present*. Ed. Raman Selden. London: Longman, 1988.

de Souza, Eunice, ed. *Nine Indian Women Poets: An Anthology*. New Delhi: Oxford UP, 1997.

Dwivedi, A.N. ed. "Suniti Namjoshi: Art and Artifice in her Work." *Papers on Indian Writing in English*. 2nd ed. Vol. 1. New Delhi: Atlantic, 2001. 210-22.

Gaur, Rashmi. *Women's Writings: Some Facets*. New Delhi: Sarup, 2003.

Goel, Savita "Suniti Namjoshi's *Feminist Fables*: A Minor Feminist Classic." *Indian Women Writers: Critical Perspective*. Ed. Jaydipsinh K. Dodiya. New Delhi: Sarup, 2000. 177-82.

Graziano, Frank. "Poetry Writing Therapy and Schizophrenia: A Poet's Point of View." *Literature and Psychology*. 29.1 (1979): 49-59.

Gupta, Meenakshi. "The Girl Child: A Psychological Perspective." *The Girl Child in Twentieth Century Indian Literature*. Ed. Viney Kirpal. Delhi: Sterling, 1992. 44-52.

Iyengar, K.R. Srinivasa. *Indian Writing in English*. 5th ed. Delhi: Sterling, 1985.

Jain, Jasbir. "Suniti Namjoshi: The Dual World of Her Early Poetry." *Problems of Postcolonial Literature and Other Essays*. Ed. Jasbir Jain. Jaipur: Printwell, 1991. 109-20.

Jussawalla, Adil. "One Woman's Poetry." *Journal of South Asian Literature*. Vol. 12.1 (1983).

Kalia, Mamta. Personal Interview. 23 Mar. 2008.

_____. Interview with Eunice de Souza. *Talking Poems: Conversations with Poets*. New Delhi: Oxford UP, 1999. 57-66.

King, Bruce. *Modern Indian Poetry in English*. Delhi: Oxford UP, 1987.

Laing, R.D. "Divided Selves." 23 May 2008 <www.jesslayton.com/jessweb/Essays/Ontological%20Insecurity%20-%201995.pdf>.

Namjoshi, Suniti. *Because of India: Selected Poems and Fables*. London: Only Women, 1989.

"Oppression in Christianity." *Man and Woman: The Age Old Struggle*. Oracle Think Quest: Education Foundation. 23 Dec. 2008 <http://library.thinkquest.org/07aug/01443/ fo_religion_christian.html>.

Panja, Shormistha. "Women and Literary Space." *Rethinking Indian English Literature*. Ed. U.M. Nanavati and Prafulla C. Kar. Delhi: Pencraft International, 2000. 95-102.

Pathak, R.S. "Indian Women Poets: Mapping out New Terrains." *Journal of Indian Writing in English*. 29 (July 2001): 14-26.

Saha, Subhas Chandra. *Modern Indo-Anglian Love Poetry*. Calcutta: Writers Workshop, 1971.

Sheshadri, Vijayalakshmi. *The New Woman in Indian English Women Writers since the 1970s*. Delhi: B.R., 1995.

Singh, Kanwar Dinesh. *Feminism and Postfeminism: The Context of Modern Indian Women Poets Writing in English*. New Delhi: Sarup, 2004.

Vijayasree, C. *Suniti Namjoshi: The Artful Transgressor*. Jaipur: Rawat, 2001.

Suniti Namjoshi's Poems: Striking a Different Note

As illustrated through the earlier chapters the poems written by contemporary Indian women poets express their deep dissatisfaction with the given world and order of things, and their realization of the need for a transformational change which leaves them perplexed and baffled. In fact, they seem to believe that there is no precise and final answer to the dilemmas of life. As a result, their restless and persistent mind that questions, probes and covets starts articulating the inner conflict. Loneliness and insecurity, social realities and life's sorrows, and the crisis of identity have become the central themes of their poetry.

The same frustration and dissatisfaction can be seen in the poetry of Suniti Namjoshi. She strikes a different note from other contemporary poets taken up for study, as her schizophrenic identity results not only from the attempt to resolve her tensions as a woman or a feminist writer, but also as a lesbian and a diasporic writer. In an interview with Christine Croyden, Namjoshi expresses how her mother disapproves of her freedom, "She has never been particularly happy about that I'm a writer, or, a lesbian feminist. She sees these as notoriety, tarnishing the good name of the family" (1).

Suniti Namjoshi comes out openly and boldly as a lesbian and considers her defiance of social norms as a counter-attack on gender exploitation. By virtue of her lack of sexual ties with man and of her freedom from conventional heterosexual commitments, especially marriage, a lesbian is always placed sociologically in a situation of great freedom. Lesbian theorists argue that by rejecting stereotypes about women, these women can think radically and profoundly about the possibility of social change with reference to gender arrangements.

In the early 1970s, the concept "woman identified woman" was an important lesbian slogan. According to lesbian theorists, a lesbian was a woman who believed in the primacy of women. "'Lesbian' was a source of an alternative model of female identity, not simply a choice of sexual activity (Radicalesbianisms, 1973)" (Qtd. Humm 164). Luce Irigaray argues that "lesbian" necessarily opposes the constructions imposed by heterosexuality and represents an alternative sexual discourse. Monique Wittig ends "The Straight Mind" with this sentence: "Lesbians are not women" (32) because the sign "woman" carries with it too many constructions and associations. According to him, "it is oppression that creates sex and not the contrary" (6). Thus, he observes:

> Lesbianism is the only concept I know of which is beyond the categories of sex (woman and man), because the designated subject (lesbian) is not a woman, either economically, or politically, or ideologically. For what makes a woman is a specific social relation to a man, a relation that we have previously called servitude, a relation which implies personal and physical obligation as well as economic obligation . . . a relation which lesbians escape by refusing to become or to stay heterosexual. (Qtd. Calhoun)

For Freud the question of lesbian desire is particularly problematic. According to him: "the maturing of feminine eroticism requires change from the clitorid stage to the vaginal stage, a change symmetrical with that which transfers to the father the love the little girl has felt for her mother." (Beauvoir 426)

However, various causes may check this developmental process; the woman may not become resigned to her "castrated" state, hiding from herself the absence of the penis and remaining fixed on her mother, for whom she is ever seeking substitute.

In Adler's view, this arrest of development is not an accident, passively suffered: "it is desired by the subject who, through the will to power, deliberately rejects her mutilation and seeks to identify herself with the male while refusing his domination. . . . Homosexuality can be for woman a mode of flight from her situation or a way of accepting it." (Qtd. Beauvoir 426)

Queer theory which is grounded in gender and sexuality is helpful in understanding any abnormality and deviation from normal sexual behaviour. This theory gives rise to a debate whether sexual orientation is natural or essential to a person, or if sexuality is mere a social construction and subject to change. David Halperin has said, "Queer is by definition whatever is at odds with the normal, the legitimate, the dominant" (Qtd. Judith Butler 3).

Given Freud's problematic views on feminine sexuality, it may seem surprising that some feminist queer theorists turn to Freud for a theory of lesbian sexuality. Freud's "notion of disavowal suggests that sexuality and psychic life are not just the result of the repression of internal drive force but also the result of negotiating external reality and social pressures" (Oliver 1). This view denies the fact that there is any normal or natural sexuality. Sexuality, however, is formed as a result of interplay between internal and external, between body and cultures, and between fantasy and reality. Once we allow that a combination of forces produce sexuality, we can imagine multitudes of possible sexualities; and concepts of normal sexuality or natural sexuality become suspicious disciplinary techniques used to serve very specific social power structures, like patriarchy.

According to Teresa de Lauretis, a queer theorist, when culture cannot provide a positive female body image for the girl as she develops into a woman, she finds fetish substitutes in order to compensate for the missing desirable female body. Kelly Oliver explains it in the following words:

> When she is made to feel bad about her body, when she is told that she is not feminine, that her body is not desirable or lovable, when the dominant culture both tells girls that they are not feminine enough and that to be feminine is bad, then they have difficulty

> finding a positive female body-image with which to fortify their own egos and self-esteem as women. (2)

The consequence is that women have to find alternative ways to value their bodies as women.

Against Freudian theory, then, de Lauretis argues that the lesbian, unlike the heterosexual man, is not trying to find a substitute mother or a substitute for the maternal phallus, as Freud suggests. Rather, she is trying to find a desirable and lovable female body-image. She describes masculinity in lesbians not as penis envy but as an embrace of one of the few symbols of desire for women available in our culture.

Judith Butler, another queer theorist, argues that sex (male, female) is seen to cause gender (masculine, feminine) which is seen to cause desire (towards the other gender). This is seen as a kind of continuum. Her approach—inspired by Foucault—is basically to smash the supposed links between these, so that gender and desire are flexible, free-floating and not caused by other stable factors. She says: "There is no gender identity behind the expressions of gender . . . identity is performatively constituted by the very 'expressions,' that are said to be its results." (25)

On the whole, lesbianism is considered as a revolt as a lesbian woman defines herself in terms of a woman only and rejects the male definition of how she should feel, love, look and live. It puts woman on the forefront while society declares the male supremacy. It threatens male supremacy at its core. The lesbian "rejects male sexual/political domination; she defies his world, his social organization, his ideology, and his definition of her as inferior" (Bunch 83).

Thus, lesbianism is a political commitment as well. It is political because relationships between men and women are essentially political: they involve power and dominance. Since a lesbian actively rejects that relationship and chooses woman, she defies the established political system. Jill Johnston writes:

> (t)he word lesbian has expanded so much through political definition that it should no longer refer exclusively to a woman simply in

> sexual relation to another woman. . . . The word is now a generic term signifying activism and resistance and the envisioned goal of a woman committed state. (Qtd. Eisenstein 48)

Suniti Namjoshi feels so oppressed by this male-dominated socio-cultural system that reduces a woman to the status of the "Other," that "she considers compulsory heterosexuality as a repressive social structure that systematically subordinates women" (Vijayasree 26). A true woman who lives beneath the façade of male-derived identity has no value of her own as her entire value is derived from his and is worthless. She is a woman who is invisible, pathetic, inauthentic and unreal. She can define herself only through a man.

> Heterosexual society offers women a few privileges as compensation if they give up their freedom: for example, mothers are 'honored,' wives or lovers are socially accepted and given some economic and emotional security, a woman gets physical protection on the street when she stays with her man, et cetera. The privileges give heterosexual women a personal and political stake in maintaining the status quo. (Bunch 85)

On the other hand, the lesbian threatens the ideology of male supremacy by destroying the lie about female inferiority, weakness, passivity, and by denying women's "innate" need for men. While discussing their lived experience as lesbians, Suniti Namjoshi and Gillian Hanscombe in the "Introduction" of their *Flesh and Paper* write, "a lesbian woman does not inhabit the worlds that make sense to heterosexual men." They do not consider "male heterosexual literary tradition" as "universal" and say: "For us, love is not the same; sex is not the same; parenting is not the same; work is not the same; safety is not the same; respect is not the same; trust is not the same. Only death might, perhaps, be the same." (Namjoshi, *Flesh* 3)

Heterosexuality is thus a system of male ownership of a woman, participation in which is compulsory for man and especially for woman. A woman's heterosexual orientation perpetuates social, economic, emotional, and sexual dependence on and accessibility to man. To Namjoshi, being a lesbian means ending identification with heterosexuality. It means ending the personal stake in the male world so that she joins women individually and collectively, to end their oppression.

Julia Kristeva clearly takes heterosexuality to be prerequisite to kinship and to culture. Consequently, she identifies lesbian experience as the psychotic alternative, a self-loss to the acceptance of paternally sanctioned laws. She projects lesbian as "Other" to culture, and characterizes lesbian speech as the psychotic "whirl of words." This positions her within the orbit of paternal-heterosexual privilege.

> In claiming that lesbianism designates loss of self, Kristeva appears to be delivering a psychoanalytic truth about the repression necessary for individuation. . . . In other words, Kristeva prefers to explain lesbian experience as a regressive libidinal state prior to acculturation itself, rather than to take up the challenge that lesbianism offers to her restricted view of paternally sanctioned cultural laws. (Butler 118)

Though the lesbian movement is supported by a number of critics, an attempt has always been made to cripple it as the heterosexual women who are in majority snub the lesbians and their social perspectives. Male society, too, defines lesbianism as a sexual act only. The male-centred society has invented lesbianism as a label to throw at any woman who dares to be man's equal, who dares to challenge his prerogative and who dares to assert the primacy of her own needs. Similar is the situation with Suniti Namjoshi. A few critics like A.N. Dwivedi and Monika Varma accuse her poetry as mere "literary doodles" (Varma 3). Instead of understanding her position in the patriarchal society and the reason of her abhorrence for heterosexual love, Monika Varma denounces her poetry for the "absurdities like *Beauty and the Beast* or *Aphrodisiac*" and asks her "to be more careful" (6). A.N. Dwivedi while discussing her poetry states: "Namjoshi comes out as a pitiable poet in the long run, lisping in foreign tongue and alien numbers and breathing the Western air and showing unnecessary compassion for her motherland. . . . If one were to accept her version of love, as indicated in 'Beauty and the Beast,' the whole human relationship between man and woman would flounder on the rocks of ruin." (214)

Kanwar Dinesh Singh at times seems to be denouncing Namjoshi's "utterly nauseating and repulsive satire" (79) but then he supports her also by saying that her "inner self is disconcerting and conflict-ridden" because of the "painful surroundings" (80). Regarding her lesbian sensibility, he comments, "She finds some kind of recompense in lesbian gamut against the betrayal shown by her male companion/lover" (81). Rashmi Bajaj, too, seems to be justifying her lesbianism by pronouncing that she is "so much disgusted with the merely physical in love that she talks nowhere of love but always of sex in a satirical vein" (51).

Patriarchy, on the whole, has created a fear of the label of "lesbian" among women. This results in discontentment and frustration which further leads to schizophrenic identity as it is in the case of the poet. Thus, lesbianism has its own clinical associations:

> as we deepen and broaden the range of what we define as lesbian existence, as we delineate a lesbian continuum, we begin to discover the erotic in female terms as that which is . . . omnipresent in 'the sharing of joy, whether physical, emotional, psychic,' and in the sharing of work; as the empowering joy which 'makes us less willing to accept powerlessness, or those other supplied states of being which are not native to me, such as resignation, despair, self-effacement, depression, self-denial.' (Rich 27)

Anup Beniwal while discussing Namjoshi's bizarre behaviour and her schizophrenic identity supports her by saying that it is because of her "tentative exploration towards the direction of self-definition" (78).

Lesbianism is much more than a matter of an individual's sexual preference. It "is much more than the defining term for the sex of your bed partner." It is a "total life commitment to a life with women" and "an entire system of world view and life living" (Qtd. Koedt 2). The "woman-identified-woman" i.e. the lesbian commits herself to other women for political, emotional, physical and economic support. Women are important to her and she is important to herself.

According to Adrienne Rich, the "social relations of the sexes are disordered and extremely problematic, if not disabling, for women, all seek paths towards change" (24). Lesbian existence is the breaking of social taboos, and the rejection of a compulsory way of life. It is an attack on the male right to the access to women.

Suniti Namjoshi's innermost feelings and proclivities can also be observed as a lesbian-feminist writer. Her search for identity "as an Indian living and writing in a predominantly White world, as a woman working in a largely male academia, as a Hindu in an all-Christian world" (Vijayasree 52) takes her to lesbianism. A lesbian is someone who has withdrawn herself from the conventional definitions of femininity. She has "refused to buy into the limitations and restrictions placed upon her by the social expectations of acting like a 'true woman'" (Eisenstein 51).

Namjoshi's *The Jackass and the Lady* spells out her position as a lesbian writer. In this she creates the Jackass, the poetic persona, who is soon joined by many other beasts. She makes this choice because in this male-dominating society she can find only birds and beasts with whom she can identify herself, thus, rejecting all gender stereotyping. She convincingly argues: "in a humanist universe, which has been male-centred historically, women are 'the other,' together with the birds and the beasts and the rest of creation" (Namjoshi, *India* 28).

Suniti Namjoshi and Gillian Hanscombe in *Flesh and Paper* express their feelings as friends, poets, lesbians and lovers. In "Narrative Distance" this sentiment can be seen:

> Climb up here on this ready-made mountain,
> sit beside me, and watch the two women

> walking on the beach, observe their relation,
> mood and emotion, each connected to each. (1-4)

Namjoshi discards the traditional sex roles and heterosexuality as they confirm the subordination of a woman. In heterosexuality every woman is simply defined by and is the property of men with a right to her body, her services and her children. It is a system which supports male domination, instead of love and support from a male. Lesbianism, on the other hand, seems to be providing a sense of relief:

> And if the sun
> is too strong, should burn too much, will you
> walk with me to where the light is more calm
> and be in me where the seas heave and are
> serene and heave again and are themselves?
>
> ("Well, then let slip the masks" 18-22)

Lesbianism, on the other hand, celebrates the relation of one woman with another. As lesbian poet Caroline Halliday while describing lesbian eroticism states: "The lesbian erotic poem is not only about connections and explorations. It is also about celebration, about breaking taboos, naming what *is* and what *is ours*" (Qtd. Vijayasree 59). The same lesbian stance can be seen in Suniti Namjoshi's poetry. In her *Flesh and Paper* the two voices (i.e. of Suniti Namjoshi and Gillian Hanscombe) "shape a universe in which the lesbian consciousness is central. What is unusual in the sequence is the sense of equality and partnership, so that traditional barriers between speaker and listener, poet and audience, dissolve" (Namjoshi, *Flesh*). Both the women are leading a carefree life:

> One of them laughs, the other smiles; they appear
> uninhibited, careless, carefree; . . .
> They are digging in the sand,
> Then they stop, consult one another, then proceed.
> And now they are walking hand in hand;
> They are picking up pebbles, sea shells, seaweed.
>
> ("Narrative Distance" 5-6, 9-12)

She seems to consider that by rejecting heterosexuality a woman can decline secondary, derivative, or second-best to men positions. Her eve prefers to be coupled with the snake rather than remain chained to Adam and bear the badge of a fallen woman:

> Eve
> in her turn
> encircled the snake, pressing her body
> to him.
> Curious coupling, brown snake and Eve,
> caught in a twist
> of the blind green coil being Adam
> and evil and Eve. ("Her Form in Clear Water" 3-10)

She was so much disappointed with the heterosexuality that she prefers to be united with animals rather than a man. It is not that heterosexual women are evil or do not care about women. It is because the very essence, definition and nature of heterosexuality give importance to men first. Her Circe symbolizes liberation from heterosexual norms and forges possibilities of alternative sexualities:

> Circe,
> all animals adore you,
> you are all things to each
> in the tutelary garden, at the continuous feast,
> ("Homage to Circe" 27-30)

Namjoshi is an impulsive woman who wishes to act according to her inner compulsions. She wants to be a more complete and free human being than her society would permit. It is lesbianism which gives her freedom from all restrictions. She with Gillian Hanscombe feels liberated to act according to her own free will:

> We can
> —I/you can—press dreams and theories, bellies,
> breasts, hair, hips, lips; and words; all
> plaited now, until tomorrow. ("Because of India" 12-15)

Suniti Namjoshi, on the whole, is not able to accept the limitations and oppressions imposed on her by the society—the subordinate, domesticated, submissive female role. It is lesbianism only which seems to give her contentment:

> Ebb is easier than flow;
> to then fro. She
> motioned
> and she motioned back. . . .
> What drew them went unsaid;
> and they were faithful
> and content. ("I invent the movie" 23-26, 30-32)

However, the decision to be a lesbian is very difficult for a woman as most women resist a direct relationship with other women. To confront other women directly means to encounter, as in a mirror, the reality of one's own true self.

> Women resist relating on all levels to other women who will reflect their own oppression, their own secondary status, their own self-hate. For to confront other woman is finally to confront one's self—the self we have gone to such lengths to avoid. And in that mirror we know we cannot really respect and love that which we have been made to be. (Eisenstein 52)

Namjoshi's "I Give her the Rose" is an early example of Namjoshi's lesbian eroticism. The poet in the poem uses nature imagery of a rose. She seems to convey that lesbian sexuality is natural unlike the heterosexuality which is culturally conditioned:

> I give her the rose with unfurled petals.
> She smiles
> and crosses her legs.
> I give her the shell with the swollen lip.
> She laughs. I bite
> and nuzzle her breasts.
> I tell her, "Feed me on flowers
> with wide open mouths,"
> and slowly,

> she pulls down my head. (1-10)

The poem is an expression of the poet's courageous defiance—defiance of all norms. It celebrates the freedom of lesbian erotic feeling, and affirms lesbian relationships actual, physical and sexual. The same sensation can be seen in her "Well, then let slip the masks" in which the poet with her partner Gillian Hanscombe expresses her lesbian desires:

> The curve of your breast is like the curve
> of a wave: look, held, caught, each instant
> caught, the wave tipping over and we in our bower,
> the two of us sheltered, my hands on your thighs,
> your body, your back, my mouth on your mouth
> and in the hollows of your jaws and your head
> nuzzling my breasts. (7-13)

In the same poem she expresses her sexual desires with an unusual boldness and audacity and her schizophrenic behaviour as seen in her earlier poetry is put back by her significant confidence:

> Will you
> take to the sea, my darling? Will you let me caress you?
> The tips of your feet, your legs, your sex?
> Will you let my tongue caress you? Will you
> lie in my arms? Will you rest? (14-18)

But this sensation of a woman's passion for another woman is met with resistance everywhere in society. A lesbian may think that she is free since she escapes the personal oppression of an individual male/female relationship. But to the society she is still a woman. This society hates women who love women, and so, a lesbian, who escapes male-dominance in her private home, receives it doubly at the hands of male society.

Lesbianism is not only the denial of patriarchy or an act of resistance as it has always been perceived. But it is more than this. "It has of course included isolation, self-hatred, breakdown, alcoholism, suicide and intrawoman violence; we romanticize at our peril what it means to love and act against the grain, and under heavy penalties; and lesbian existence has been lived without access to any knowledge of a tradition, continuity, a social underpinning." (Rich 26)

The same is the case with Suniti Namjoshi. Though she is a lesbian, yet the oppression as a woman which she is facing under patriarchy has not ended. Her schizophrenic existence ensures that she is not leading a life according to her own free will as it is ideally supposed in case of lesbians.

Her poetry is a revelation of her rueful, unfortunate state as a poet who is silently singing the sad song of her life. The poetry is full of cynicism and disgust in the matter of love and sex as it can be seen in the following lines in her "Beauty and the Beast." The poet comments on the contemporary sexual norms and stresses:

> the complex mind
> Sees infidelity only as a symptom
> Of passion. (13-15)

The poem shows a deep sense of horror and disgust in the matter of love and sex.

Her attitude towards God is no better. The poem "Rationale" brings out in unmistakable terms "her spit and venom at the whole creation of God . . . she is out to find faults not only with the creation, but also with the creator" (Dwivedi 234):

> Perhaps creation is purely accidental? . . .
> My God is rock-faced. He does not move.
> Perhaps if you pushed, He'd topple over. (18, 23-24)

It is the patriarchal society as a whole which makes a woman so horribly pessimistic and bitingly ironical in her outlook upon life. The poet, too, has become gloomy as an outcome of the same society. She usually resorts to "a dry, ironic, and cynical tone" (Iyengar 684):

> It's a quality of the gods
> To see a creature with its back broken

And be unmoved, . . .
The gods are unafraid,
And the gods are unbroken,
And cannot love and cannot grieve.
("It's a Quality of the Gods" 1-3, 6-8)

She portrays God as cruel and sadistic.

Suniti Namjoshi's schizophrenic tendencies also emanate from her diasporic experience. Diasporic situation involves relocation not in terms of geography alone. Robin Cohen tentatively describes diasporas as communities of people living together in one country who "acknowledge that the old country—a notion often buried deep in language, religion, custom or folklore—always has some claim on their loyalty and emotions." Cohen continues: "a member's adherence to a diasporic community is demonstrated by an acceptance of an inescapable link with their past migration history and a sense of co-ethnicity with others of a similar background" (ix). The significant aspect of diaspora can be seen in socio-culture and psychological re-location.

> Individuals as well as group of people belonging to particular nation-communities in diasporic situations oscillate between two identities, two culture value systems and even two mind-sets—one belonging to the nation and the community they are migrating from and the other the nation and the community they are migrating into. (Narang vi)

The writings of a diasporic writer shift from one land to another i.e. native to the adopted one. Their works are full of memory and imaginary homelands as it is evident in the poetry of Suniti Namjoshi:

My aging beauty,
God forbid
That I hurt you.
You are a young man
With green eyes.
You are all the people I have loved.
You are beautiful, geographically,

And I love you. ("My Aging Country" 14-21)

A diasporic person lives two lives at once. He lives in two cultures simultaneously. As Avtar Brah puts it, distinct diaspora communities are created out of the "confluence of narratives" of different journeys from the "old country" to the new which create the sense of a shared history (183).

However, this particular mode of existence is not free from problems. Too often diasporas have been ghettoized and excluded from feeling they belong to the "new country," and suffered their cultural practices to be mocked and discriminated against. And the psychological movements of such persons from one state of mind to another cause dilemma, nostalgia, sense of displacement and loss, thus giving them a somewhat schizophrenic identity. "Diasporic writing raises questions regarding the definitions of 'home' and 'nation.' Schizophrenia and/or nostalgia are often the preoccupations of these writers as they seek to locate themselves in new cultures." (Trivedi 57)

In *More Poems* Suniti Namjoshi describes the loss of self-identity one experiences as a foreigner in an alien land. Throughout the volume, the theme of dislocation and diasporic living dominates. This fear of living in an alien and unfamiliar land amidst strangers can be seen in her poem "How to be a Foreigner":

First,
    You take off your clothes,
    Your titles and name
    And put on a robe,
    Sterile and clean,
    With neat black letters
    Marking THE STRANGERS.
Then,
    You walk down the street,
    Alone in fancy dress. (1-10)

In her poems "The Old Country Says" and "My Aging Country," a feeling of nostalgia can be seen. The poet is not satisfied with the predicament of her diasporic existence. Migrations, i.e. movements across borders—geographical or otherwise—can be wilful or forced. "Such migrations have resulted in building up a diasporic community who share a common sense of rootlessness, pain and agony of homelessness, experience the anxiety and turmoil in a new land and the nostalgia for their homeland." (Sharma xv)

A mood of ambivalence marks Namjoshi's poetry. Her regret with the present state of affairs can be seen in her poem "My Aging Country." Her bewilderment can be seen in the very opening lines:

> How shall I take you,
> Having no handle? (1-2)

Vijayasree asserts, "As an expatriate who is cut off from her aging country, she knows she wields no power" (39). However, her love for her home is also clearly identifiable:

> You are beautiful,
> In a blue sea. . . .
> And I love you. (4-5, 7)

The concept of home often performs an important function in our lives. It can act as a valuable means of orientation by giving us a sense of our place in the world. It tells us where we originated from and where we belong: "As an idea it [home] stands for shelter, stability, security and comfort. To be 'at home' is to occupy a location where we are welcome, where we can be with people very much like ourselves." (McLeod 210)

But this idea of home as an ambivalent location in Namjoshi's poetry shows that her identity is not fixed but stays in transition and is destined to end up in one place or another, either returning to its roots or disappearing through partial assimilation in a hermeneutic "fusion." She seems to be caught between a nativist traditionalism and a postcolonial metropolitan assimilation, i.e. the migrant culture of the "in-between" according to Homi Bhaba. "New diasporas have relocated the Self there and the

Other here, and consequently borders and boundaries have been confounded. And the flow has become at once homogenizing and heterogenizing." (Dirlik 352)

The imaginary home brings fragmentation, discontinuity and displacement for the migrants. At the same time living in diaspora which connotes living in forced or voluntary exile leads to severe identity confusion and problems. It further leads to identification with and alienation from old and new cultures and homelands. In *Shame*, Salman Rushdie says:

> All migrants leave their pasts behind although some try to pack it into bundles and boxes—but on the journey something seeps out of the treasured mementoes and old photographs, until even their owners fail to recognize them, because it is the fate of migrants to be stripped of history, to stand naked among the scorn of strangers upon whom they see the rich clothing, the brocades of continuity and the eyebrows of belonging. (Qtd. Mandal 42)

Speaking of Indian migrants, Rushdie writes: "our physical alienation from India almost inevitably means that we will not be capable of reclaiming precisely the thing that was lost; that we will, in short, create fictions, not actual cities or villages, but invisible ones, imaginary homelands, Indias of the mind." (10)

The same experience recurs in Namjoshi's poem "The Elsewhere Fish." Loss and longing are very poignantly expressed here. The poet is unable to bridge the gap between the country she left behind and the country of adoption. And to live in the world unperceived, it appears to her like "burning precious fuel." And she says:

> It seems to me,
> That I, in my element of blue,
> And you in your foreign country,
> Are being cheated unawares. (20-23)

Migrants may well live in new places, but they can be considered not to belong there and disqualified from thinking of the new land as their home. "Instead, their home is seen to exist elsewhere, back across the border" (McLeod 212). The same is the situation with Suniti Namjoshi:

> I would need wings, seven league boots
> And a clock of invisibility
> To come to you. ("The Elsewhere Fish" 1-3)

Namjoshi in her poems also expresses the predicament of a country which has lost its people:

> The old country says
> My young people are all out,
> Voyaging through strange lands. ("The Old Country says" 1-3)

The country asks its people who have left it "Have I not brought them up well?" (7). For her "the two countries become the two countries of mind, of belonging or not belonging, of being left out and being involved" (Jain 116).

The past which she had spent in her country fills her with a feeling of nostalgia. In her little poem "Letter" this sentiment can be observed. Her feeling to communicate across the temporal and spatial distance has been asserted in this poem. The poet says:

> And I open my mind thus and thus
> And say, 'if it should please you,
> Come and spend little time with me.' (14-16)

Sometimes everything appears hollow and worthless to Suniti Namjoshi and she gets perplexed and baffled by the contradictions that mark human existence:

> Life is an exercise in living
> I'm sick and needn't say
> Anything that makes sense at all.
> ("Sick in a Strange Country" 17-19)

Loneliness, isolation and marginalization are also seen in her poem "When I Cry":

> When I cry my tears trickle into brine
> You never saw me cry.

> That was sea-water the wind carried off. (1-3)

The people of the diasporic groups remain in conflictual situation—now looking back, now the gaze fixed straight ahead. They want to practise their own culture and value system and remain reluctant to imbibe new-ones. As a result they remain disappointed and alienated in their new situation. Sometime extreme states of conflict emerge and turn these individuals into "cultural schizophrenics" and they become "victims of maladjustment, haunted by as it were Hamlet's dilemma—to be or not to be" (Narang xiii).

The poetry of Suniti Namjoshi belongs to the in-between space. Her poetry like any other diasporic writer is a revelation of her inner uncertainties, clashes and dilemmas. She doesn't seem to be happy with the situation she has been put in by the circumstances. She is residing in America but her dissatisfaction with the materialism of America is clearly visible in her poems:

> I asked the New York Bird whether he'd prefer
> To be a parrot, but the New York Bird said,
> 'I was planned and made by American man.
> Parrots are purely accidental.' ("New York Bird" 12-15)

The poet's discontentment with America's capacity to commodify everything is noticeable. Her fragmented psyche and alienated existence in a foreign land cause discontentment with the situation. She expresses her deep disapproval with the system. So much so that she ends her poem "New York Bird" in the following manner:

> In accordance with my duty
> I caught the New York Bird and opened
> His heart to learn what made him tick.
> Now we have a factory for New York Birds
> Though two inch beaks are no longer worn. (17-21)

In her poem "Alwin Ailey," she has brought out the racial violence prevalent in America. Negroes and whites danced together a ballet dance in which White devils kicked the Negro ladies out. The poet says:

> If everyone was taught
> To be a ballet dancer,
> Life would be so graceful
> And cruel. (5-8)

Violence, alienation, racial prejudice and discrimination prevalent in America make the poet's "eye floods with tears" ("A Problem" 1). Her despair is:

> Can a body hurt a body? (2)

Jaswant Guzder and Meenakshi Krishna in "Mind the Gap: Diaspora Issues of Indian Women in Psychotherapy" express: "Diaspora women, with origins in Hindu Indian culture spaces, are seeking psychotherapy to address mental health and personal identity issues within the North American context" (121).

Though, on one hand, Namjoshi's poems are filled with nostalgia for her motherland and discontentment with the materialism of the foreign land, but at the same time India of her poetry becomes "the India of poverty and pettiness, of old age and lost lustre" (Dwivedi 219):

> You lie there,
> Smiling, lazy, wicked,
> Unashamed of yourself,
> Lazy in a blue sea.
> You really don't think
> You might smarten yourself. ("My Aging Country" 8-13)

Thus, most often, Suniti Namjoshi's poetry becomes an expression of her lesbian desires and diasporic experiences. Namjoshi is the first Indian woman writer to have openly declared her sexual preference as a lesbian, and "has since held that kind of sexual life one chooses to lead is a purely personal matter, where an individual's autonomy should neither be checked nor curtailed" (Vijayasree 26). She doesn't want to give up in this man-made society and as a result her poetry reveals the schizophrenic battle within her divided self.

Works Cited

Bajaj, Rashmi. *Women Indo-Anglian Poets: A Critique*. New Delhi: Asian, 1996.

Beauvoir, Simone de. *The Second Sex*. Trans. H.M. Parshley. New York: Vintage, 1952.

Beniwal, Anup. "Identity, Experience, Aesthetic: Indian Women's Poetry in English." *Occasional Papers* (March 1999): 71-95.

Brah, Avtar. *Cartographies of Diaspora: Contesting Identities*. New York: Routledge, 1997.

Bunch, Charlotte. "Lesbians as Revolt." *Feminist Theory Reader: Local and Global Perspectives*. Ed. Carole R. McCann and Seung-Kyung Kim. New York: Routledge, 2003. 83-87.

Butler, Judith. *Gender Trouble: Feminism and the Subversion of Identity*. New York: Routledge, 2007.

Calhoun, Cheshire. "Separating Lesbian Theory from Feminist Theory." *Feminist Theory Reader: Local and Global Perspectives*. Ed. Carole R. McCann and Seung-Kyung Kim. 334-52.

Cohen, Robin. *Global Diasporas: An Introduction*. London: UCL Press, 1997.

Croyden, Christine. Interview with Suniti Namjoshi. *Hecate's Australian Women's Book Review*. Ed. Brook Barbara. 15 May 2007 <http://www.emsah.uq.edu.au/awsr/recent/8.html>.

Dirlik, Arif. "The Post-Colonial Aura: Third World Criticism in the Age of Global Capitalism." *Critical Inquiry* 20 (Winter 1994): 352-53.

Dwivedi, A.N., ed. *Papers on Indian Writing in English*. 2nd ed. Vol. 1. New Delhi: Atlantic, 2001.

Eisenstein, Hester. *Contemporary Feminist Thought*. London: Unwin, 1984.

Guzder, Jaswant and Meenakshi Krishna. "Mind the Gap: Diaspora Issues of Indian Women in Psychotherapy." *Psychology and Developing Societies*. 17.2 (2005): 121-138. 24 Aug. 2008 <http://pds.sagepud.com/cgi/content/abstract/17/2/12>.

Humm, Maggie. *Practising Feminist Criticism: An Introduction.* London: Prentice Hall, 1995.

Iyengar, K.R. Srinivasa. *Indian Writing in English.* 5th ed. Delhi: Sterling, 1985.

Jain, Jasbir. "Suniti Namjoshi: The Dual World of Her Early Poems." *Problems of Postcolonial Literature and Other Essays.* Ed. Jasbir Jain. Jaipur: Printwell, 1991.

Judith Butler. 26 Nov. 2008 <http://www.theory.org.uk/ctr-butl.htm>.

Koedt, Anne. *Lesbianism and Feminism.* 16 June 2006 <http://www.cwluherstory.com/CWLUArchive/lesbianfeminisx.html>.

Mandal, Somdatta. "The 'Desh-Pradesh' Syndrome: Texts and Contexts of Diasporic Indian Writing in English." *Contemporary Diasporic Literature: Writing History, Culture, Self.* Ed. Manjit Inder Singh. Delhi: Pencraft, 2007. 37-48.

McLeod, John. *Beginning Postcolonialism.* Manchester: Manchester UP, 2000.

Namjoshi, Suniti. *Because of India: Selected Poems.* London: Only Women, 1989.

Namjoshi, Suniti, and Gillian Hanscombe. *Flesh and Paper.* Charlottestown, Canada: Ragweed, 1986.

Narang, Harish. Foreword. *Mapping Migrations: Perspectives on Diasporic Fiction.* By Charu Sharma. xi-xiv.

Oliver, Kelly. "Lesbian Desire and Fetishism." *APA Newsletters* 99.2 (Spring 2000). 7 Aug. 2008 <http://mail.google.com/mail/?ui=1&attid=0.7&disp=vah&view=att&th=11b9b6c75fd3165e>.

Rich, Adrienne. "Compulsory Heterosexuality and Lesbian Existence." *Feminist Literary Theory: A Reader.* Ed. Mary Eagleton. UK: Blackwell, 1994. 24-29.

Rushdie, Salman. *Imaginary Homelands: Essays and Criticism 1981-1991.* Minneapolis: University of Minnesota Press, 1996.

Sharma, Charu. Introduction. *Mapping Migrations: Perspectives on Diasporic Fiction.* New Delhi: Books Plus, 2006. xv-xviii.

Singh, Kanwar Dinesh. *Feminism and Postfeminism: The Context of Modern Indian Women Poets Writing in English.* New Delhi: Sarup, 2004.

Trivedi, Deepkumar Jayprakash. "Identity Crisis in Indian Diaspora." *Re-Markings.* 7.2 (2008): 56-59.

Varma, Monika. *Facing Four: A Critical Opinion on the Poetry of Suniti Namjoshi, Gauri Deshpande, Kamala Das, Bharati Sarabhai.* Calcutta: Writers Workshop, 1973.

Vijayasree, C. *Suniti Namjoshi: The Artful Transgressor.* Jaipur: Rawat, 2001.

Wittig, Monique. *The Straight Mind and Other Essays.* Boston: Becon, 1992.

Conclusion

The poetry written by contemporary Indian women poets is generally considered to be revealing "the growth of feminine poetic consciousness" on one hand and on the other hand "the changing position of women in Indian society" (Hasan 20). However, after a thorough examination of the selected works of the women poets taken up for study, it has been found that the contemporary Indian women poets are still in the midst of dualities, because of the dilemma between what they want to do and what they are expected to do. The ensuing conflicts that arise in their unconscious minds and their ultimate resignation to their fate result in the development of schizophrenic tendencies in them. Although the seven poets belong to different parts of the country, yet they share the same dissatisfaction with the given world order, and their inner desire of the need for a transformation in the situation of women leaves them perplexed and baffled. In their similarities and disparities, all of them have unconscious repressed desires which surface in the form of a symptom or somatic (physical) disturbance: gestures, dreams, slips of the tongue, nervous tics, delusions, hallucinations and so on. Their poetry reveals the psyche of Indian women in general—women who are still caught on the horns of quandary—whether to assert independence at the cost of values cultivated over centuries or to be lost in the limbo of apathy, drudgery and slavery.

In their early poems, all the poets find themselves caught between the conflict of tradition-bound self and the self looking for freedom and independence. They register their protest and resentment against a culture and society which gives preference to male children. They reveal acute awareness of the tragic fate which comes with the feeling of being born as a woman. Eunice de Souza has expressed this sentiment in "De Souza Prabhu." The feeling of disability is so deeply ingrained in a woman's mind that she starts considering herself as a member of the category of "lame ducks" (14).

The poetry of these poets shows that the cultural presumptions of the people which identify home-making and child-bearing with femininity lead to an inevitable effect on a girl's personality and identity. The lessons on flexibility, adjustment and submissiveness hinder the development of strong opinions and commitments in a girl. The bewilderment of a growing girl who is coaxed and conditioned into stereotypical roles has been delineated by these poets.

When some of them were interviewed in person, the poets spoke about the cramping effect of marriage on their lives and this is reflected in their poems. Married life has given them unbearable tensions. They cannot open up their hearts even to their parents and near ones. The reality of Indian marriage, wifehood and motherhood has been exposed by these poets. Mamta Kalia admits: "I am a great fool/ To think that marriage is a bliss" ("I am a Great Fool" 1-2).

The poets have shown their resentment against the conventional practice by which at the time of marriage, a girl is made to shift from her parental home into the unfamiliar, initially forbidding environment, of her in-laws' place. She then begins to live without the love and support of precisely those persons whom she needs most in this transitional phase. Sunita Jain says:

> I felt pain when I came to my 'sasural' as I became someone's 'bhabhi,' 'chachi,' and 'mami' at the tender age of 18. I felt as if I don't have any identity of my own. It was a big shock—breaking away all the relationships from the past and building new ones in just a short span of one day.

The marital relationship seems to be a setback to these poets because the husbands are typically patriarchal in their viewpoints. Besides marriage, the other cause of discontentment is kitchen drudgery which has often been condemned by the women poets. Sunita Jain feels burdened by the household chores like "years of washing dishes" which gives her a "creasing forehead" and "vague" eye that sees nothing. "When the husband leaves in the morning she feels relieved from a suffocating atmosphere" (Bajaj 61).

Mamta Kalia's poetry also presents how the daily household chores and drudgery has brought ennui and sickness to her life. All romance has gone out of life, and her state at the age of 37 is that she sleeps with a "headache" and wakes up with a "backache." The complex joint family system is another major factor that is responsible for filling the life of a woman with tension and fear, frustration and suspicion. Her poem "After Eight Years of My Marriage" has presented how this family system in India proves to be a catastrophe and disaster for a woman. In an interview in person she said:

> I still remember when I used to cook, I used to dust 'atta' from my clothes and get into the car and move to college. I also couldn't leave my family hungry. . . . The progressive career of a girl is hampered in marriage because a girl may be expected to be at a certain place at a certain time by our traditional family.

The husbands have also turned out to be unworthy for these poets because they still adhere to conservative practices and ideas. Thus, the irony of an Indian girl's coming-of-age can be seen in their poetry.

Even the relationship of these poets with their children has not been gratifying. It is very difficult for the poets to adjust with their own children as the latter develop their own individuality and wish to maintain it, thus wanting no parental interventions in their lives. Mamta Kalia and Sunita Jain's poetry discusses this attitude of the children and the woman's unhappiness with it. Sunita Jain while talking about her daughter says:

> I listen to her thin babble
> of welcome
> as her hard eye

on my chore-worn face
frowns
on this intrusion
in her privacy. ("The Occasional Visit" 8-14)

This poetry written by contemporary women poets also reveals the sexual harassment which a woman faces at the workplace. Moreover, the poets are not happy in a situation which demands that they bear the double burden of house and keeping jobs. At home their work is seldom recognized and at their workplace they are never treated as independent-minded individuals as their poems illustrate and here the crisis deepens. Simone de Beauvoir aptly points out that the secondary position of a woman is not imposed of necessity by natural feminine characteristics but rather by strong environmental forces of social traditions and education which have been under the control of men. Beauvoir asserts: "She [woman] is defined and differentiated with reference to man and not he with reference to her; she is the incidental, the inessential as opposed to the essential. He is the Subject, he is the Absolute—she is the Other." (xvi)

Though such patriarchal pressures have constituted traumas for the women poets, an increasing awareness of the injustice done to them has slowly made them raise their voice against inequality and oppression. They have not remained silent in such a situation. The secondary status attributed to them has made the quest for identity a prime concern. A growing sense of self-identity resulting in a clamour for recognition is evident in their poetry.

This new generation of women poets has emerged as "unafraid, motivated, clear sighted" (de Souza 6), partly due to the influence of feminist ideologies which have been discussed in Chapter 2. The poets are increasingly conscious of their identity crisis at various levels of being and have tried to express their gender related crises. While studying her "Tribute to Papa" Mamta Kalia has been discussed as a rebellious daughter as when she says:

> These days I am seriously thinking of
> disowning you, Papa. (23-24)

As she states in an interview:

> I was a rebel like in the sense my parents were very methodical people. . . . I wanted to bite. I wanted to bite everybody. I wanted to express myself in the worst of words. It was very dissatisfactory. As a young girl of 27, I was not happy at all. I had to live a life which I never wanted.

Her bitter resentment with the order of things which was expressed during the interview and the bitterness observed in her poetry exemplify the hot-blooded nature of the feelings that emerge as a distinct feature of the contemporary women's poetry.

Though these poets pronounce their discontentment loudly, they seem to be shocked and frustrated at the same time because the freedom and independence they crave for are denied to them. The conflict in their minds between feminist leanings and tradition-bound roles has left them bewildered and perplexed. The poetry surfaces as an expression of the psychic striptease of a woman who is denied what she hungers after. The poets are revealing their dilemma without inhibitions. Gauri Deshpande has put across the predicament of a woman in one of her poems:

> You sight me glimpsingly
> and won't wait too long,
> with a half-smile in your raised eyebrow
> will leave me between shores
> and walk off. ("Poem" 11-15)

The new generation of poets has raised questions but is unable to get any definite answer. Their poetry suggests that there are no neat and final answers to the dilemmas of life. Simone de Beauvoir explicates this situation of a woman: "The situation of woman is that she—a free and autonomous being like all creatures—nevertheless finds herself living in a world where men compel her to assume the status of the Other." (29)

Suniti Namjoshi also questions the reasons for women's silence in spite of all that they have to bear:

> Was it courage or fear that kept us silent
> Watching the dragonfly over the water?
>
> ("The Head of Rose" 10-11)

In her disillusionment she reconsiders the man-woman relationship and ultimately decides to live without a man.

The poets have revolted against establishments of all sorts—the bonds of marriage, family and society—from which they wish to flee. Lalitha Venkateswaran in "Debit" has expressed this desire: "I would escape your circle if I could" ("Debit" 1). But this desire for freedom has ultimately led to a conflict in the minds of the poets. Eunice de Souza while defying the norms on one side has been found to be suppressing her inner desires and trying to smile on the other hand. The psychoanalytic feminist perspective has assisted in assessing this conflict between the tendency to rebel and to conform to the norms and the resultant schizophrenia.

The "double-voiced discourse" and the "muted story" of these women poets have been interpreted as their schizophrenic existence as discussed in the present project. Their "wild zone becomes the place for the revolutionary women's language" (Showalter 324). It is this zone that makes women reside inside and outside the male tradition simultaneously.

Thus, one consequence which has come into view due to this kind of inequity in their minds is a heightened female frustration and depression under the pressures of patriarchy, together with a generally pronounced conflict and bewilderment which has ultimately resulted in their developing a schizophrenic identity. C. Vijayasree while commenting on the poetry of Suniti Namjoshi rightly points out that her poetry presents "schizophrenic battle within the divided self" (Vijayasree 37). The characteristics of a schizophrenic person i.e. odd behaviour, unusual tearfulness, deep sadness, suicidal attempts, delusions, hallucinations and disorderly thinking have frequently been referred to by contemporary Indian women poets. Very often the poets behave in the manner of schizophrenics.

The extent of the frustration of these women with the existing system can be gauged by the fact that they do not hesitate to question the very existence of love. Lalitha Venkateswaran in one of her prominent poems asks:

> Why do I love you, if at all;
> How much is it, and where is it;
> Is it seasonal, or evergreen;
> What are its exits and its entrances. ("Declarations" 2-5)

Love and marriage are not the ultimate sources of fulfillment in the lives of women. Debjani Chatterjee expresses the agony of a woman who is married and yet, lonely; she has lost her freedom in an alien country, while marriage has not given her much:

> You are married and yet single—naturally!
> Are you not British and yet black?
> Learn to sing of thwarted love and broken home.
> ("Primary Purpose" 42-44)

A melancholic tone, and a deep feeling of the oppressions and tensions faced by women in society can be witnessed in whatever these poets say, even their laughter is underlined with sadness/ sorrow:

> I laugh till tears
> Ran down my cheeks, stumbling
> From the bed, laughing;
> Till tears ran down my cheeks. ("Only a Joke" 27-30)

All these dualities have left the poets sad, lonely and empty and their poetry as a result has become poetry of failure rather than that of success and self-assertion. The poets are tortured by existential factors like restlessness, meaninglessness, fear, pain, sufferings and sorrows. Sunita Jain has spent:

> Many the days that cried for respite
> Many the nights that would not go to sleep.
> ("I Don't Know, Love, if You Caused" 4-5)

Eunice de Souza even does not hesitate to confess her suicidal tendencies and her delusion which are again the foremost characteristics of schizophrenia:

> the whole world
> was trying to rip me up. ("Autobiographical" 23-24)

In her distress Gauri Deshpande says, "The rush of passing days disturbs me" ("Marks: 1" 6). Vacillating between passivity and rebellion she reflects the frustration and disappointment which lead to her schizophrenic existence.

The bizarre attitude of Mamta Kalia is also an illustration of the schizophrenic nature of these poets' existence. As mentioned earlier in "Compulsions" she wants to "pick" her "nose/ in a public place" (1-2), she wants to "sit" in her "office chair" (3) with her "feet up" (4), she wants to "slap the boy/ who makes love in a café" (5-6). Not only this, she also wants "to pay Sunday visits/ totally undressed" (9-10), indicating behaviour which sounds a bit abnormal and is actually rebellious.

Although the contemporary Indian women poets are not schizophrenics in the medical sense of the term as we uphold the creation of art something created by the whole psyche, by the conscious and the unconscious and we accept that a temporary regression from the world of rational consciousness may be a necessary moment in poetic creation. "An oscillation between regression and full vigilance . . . results in a creative product" (Graziano 51). So the poetic genius may sometimes be described as eccentric. The other question is: "If the writer is neurotic in his themes, how is it that his work is intelligible to his readers?" (Welleck 82). The poets studied also reveal a bitter discontentment with reality which results in dualities of thoughts. Moreover, as Nayantara Sahgal says, "We are all somewhat divided selves" (104) and according to Pascal, "Men are so necessarily mad, that not to be mad would amount to another form of madness" (Qtd. Foucault xi).

The schizophrenic existence of these poets is reflected not only in their similarities but in disparities also. The poets have used different methods to tackle the passivity imposed on them and the ensuing stridency in their tone and behaviour. Mamta Kalia has adopted irony, ordinariness and confessional mode in her poetry to express her anger and dissatisfaction with her life.

Gauri Deshpande has opted for love poetry which is different because of its free, frank and uninhibited portrayal of sex. A man excites her "yearnings" and "unseen, unknown images" but at the same time his actual physical presence and closeness make her feel disgusted with "bareness of your presence" ("Poems in Winter" 26). Thus, while revelling in the physical act, Gauri Deshpande expresses her contempt and distaste for sexual pleasure. Her poetry, as a result, gets suffused with personal anguish and dilemma and the psychological matrix of her experience makes her swim deep in the sea of pessimism and dispiritedness.

Suniti Namjoshi is a poet gifted with ironic perception and wit. In order to express her strong sense of discontentment with the values prevalent in the society, she is deconstructing the allusions in her poems. Her situation gets further complicated and even more distinct because she is not just a woman poet but also a lesbian and a diasporic writer. Her schizophrenic identity is the result of the attempt to resolve her tensions not only as a woman or a feminist writer, but also as a lesbian and a diasporic writer. It is the lesbianism which has given her some recompense. She has considered it: "a purely personal matter, where an individual's identity should neither be curtailed nor checked. She views compulsory heterosexuality as a repressive social structure that systematically subordinates women and reduces them to the status of 'the other' in a male dominated socio-cultural systems" (Vijayasree 26). She along with Gillian Hanscombe feels:

> It is not that your country is my country
> or that where you lead I always follow,
> though I do follow and follow freely.
> In the land of the patriarchs
> we walk together ("It is not that your country" 1-5)

In her poems, the tone of nostalgia which is very strong has also given rise to a schizophrenic battle. The fears of living in an alien land and amidst strangers are voiced by her. Such poems present the feeling of distance, separation, loss and longing.

Like Namjoshi, Debjani Chatterjee's schizophrenic identity gets revealed in her diasporic existence. In her distress which emerges because of being an immigrant, she says:

> No matter what your generation,
> You will always be an immigrant. ("Primary Purpose" 3-4)

While moving from one place to another, she considers herself, "imprisoned" in her "time-machine" ("Distance" 16). Moreover, she is quite aware of the predicament of women in general as she says:

> I was that woman who roused a nation
> And was burnt so many times at so many stakes.
> ("I Was that Woman" 47-48)

Although Lalitha Venkateswaran, unlike the other women poets included in the project, has been brought up in a comparatively open environment as she says:

> Secure in my own world,
> I knew only triumph. ("Chitrangada" 5-6)

yet the situation is no less frightening and distressing to her:

> After many summers, winters, rains,
> For me this spring is full of tears. (18-19)

She has written poems which are highly intense and personal as compared to other women poets.

The anger and resentment against the Goan-Catholic community emerges as one of the distinct features of Eunice de Souza's schizophrenic existence. The annoyance and fury which is prevalent in many of her poems has been discussed at length during the course of study. In her case, as in the case of Suniti Namjoshi, schizophrenic identity can be concluded distinct and different from other women writers taken up for study because it deals with the religious oppression she faces.

Sunita Jain's poetry reveals her thirst for being truly loved. However, this love appears to be self-love in the ultimate analysis. "The women poets want it to be a means of self-fulfillment and self-actualization. Self expands and seeks meaning in a broader frame and love is sought to be a means of that expansion" (Bajaj 59). In her quest for being truly loved, she says:

> You who breathe through me
> Breathe some more. ("You who breathe through me" 13-14)

In her love poems it is companionship and togetherness which are more important than the physical act of love. She like an average Indian woman seeks emotional satisfaction and involvement of heart and considers sex as important but only as an expression of love.

During the survey, the cause of the schizophrenic identity of the poets has not been found to be a biological one. It is the study of psychoanalytical feminism which confirms that in the process of growth and development of a woman in the society, these schizophrenic characteristics are partly a result of unconscious sexual desires which have been repressed. It has shown that gender is constructed; it is not just wholly natural, but produced.

Almost all the poets taken up for the project have ultimately resigned themselves to the prevailing situation as is reflected in their later poetry. Their earlier defiance has been replaced with compliance and acceptance of the constraints. A woman like Sunita Jain who refused to be straitjacketed in the world of categorizers, now seems to have learnt to live in this male-dominated society. Earlier so rebellious, she now confesses:

> I think a woman has always been an emancipated being. Since Stone Age she is working with men. These days a desire has been created for equality and emancipation. These are the words which have been put into our minds. A woman can be totally emancipated

> but at the cost of her family and children. . . . The word 'emancipation' has been blown up out of proportion by social activists. (Jain)

Though shocked and frustrated at the loss of freedom which she had always craved yet having no alternative, she now tries to accept an entirely appalling situation. This resignation to defeat is another schizophrenic characteristic.

Similar is the predicament of Suniti Namjoshi who is tired of the emotional wanderings attempting to explore an identity and freedom and has also learnt how to suffer in this society:

> Merciful God, you taught us the meaning of guilt
> And the world taught us how to trouble ourselves . . .
> We have learnt how to suffer. ("The Lesson" 1-2, 5)

Eunice de Souza also acknowledges that women "finally learn/ to claim nothing" ("Aubade" 10-11). She now wants to give up her earlier resentment against all established orders and wants to go with what her hair-dresser says, "take it as it comes" ("Bequest" 8). This loss of interest in life which has been perceived in the later poetry of Eunice de Souza is also a characteristic of schizophrenia.

The case of Gauri Deshpande is not much different because she ultimately finds resignation to be the only solution to her tensions and disquiet. She loses her interest in life to such an extent that she has even shed her desire for freedom and has chosen compliance.

Even the very rebellious Mamta Kalia later on accepts her destiny as a woman living in the male-dominated society. She admits that she is a weak person. She has also learnt this fact that to remain happy it is better "to flatter" a male and to go along with the patriarchal society than to defy the norms:

> But ever since I learnt to flatter
> I was happy. ("What Could He Do" 20-21)

Hence, the new generation of Indian poets has tried to discover its own voice by developing its sensibilities. The themes have related to life in all its aspects. The poetry has struggled to break the boundaries of tradition while describing the conflict between the old and the new, and it has endeavoured to express the desire of a woman to break free of the bonds that have restricted her since times immemorial. However, the crisis a woman faces is that the entrenched patriarchal structure is still controlling and restricting her life in one way or the other. It still considers that she is someone's daughter, wife or mother, minus her own personality. The poetry of these poets taken up for the project reveals the frustrations and tensions of a woman because of the patriarchal structure and the discrepancy between the way she wants to behave and the way she is made to behave. An in-depth study of these poets further reveals the difference between their early and later poetry. In most of the cases, the point which emerges is the hiatus between their inner desire for a transformation of socio-cultural reality and the deep dissatisfaction with the given world order. This leaves them perplexed and baffled and ultimately they are reduced to a state of resignation from an earlier defiant stance. This bewilderment and ultimate resignation bestow upon them the schizophrenic characteristics.

Though the poets have not given any comprehensive vision or philosophy, but their poetry reveals similar divided selves and schizophrenic existence. Rarely have these poets shown their concerns with social evils like purdah, sexual crimes, ill-treatment of widows, Sati, bride-burning, infanticide, and female-foeticide—all of which make woman a victim. The prime concern of these poets is their individual self—the self which is divided and tortured as a result of the societal pressures—which mould their psyche and make them conform to the norms. These contemporary women poets are "sensitive persons," and as Rashmi Bajaj declares, "the callous society turns sensitive persons into schizophrenics" (268) has been proved in this study.

However, this schizophrenia which generally appears to be a morbid and defeatist thing—offering no hope and direction for future—becomes, for these women poets and others in general, a methodical attempt for the dismemberment of the given identities, images, equations and constructs. It has led to reconfiguring the subjectivities and charting newer modes of self-actualization. Deleuze and Guattari describe unconscious desire as flowing between two poles: the schizophrenic and the paranoiac. "In bodies whose flow is towards the schizophrenic pole, there is a desire to deterritorialize. In bodies where the flow of desire is towards the paranoiac, there is a desire to territorialize. Schizoanalysis asks us to deterritorialize the Oedipal structure" (Smith 1).

The same is the case with these poets. The unconscious desires of these poets flowing towards the schizophrenic pole, have a desire to deterritorialize i.e. a desire to move away from a rigidly imposed hierarchical context, which seeks to package things into discreet categorized units with singular coded meanings or identities, towards a rhizomatic zone of multiplicity and fluctuant identity, where meanings and operations flow freely between said things, resulting in a dynamic, constantly changing set of interconnected entities with fuzzy individual boundaries.

The age of reason demands secrecy in order to avoid scandal and confines all sorts of irregular and abnormal people. However, madness is equally important as it not only organizes the unreason, but also reveals it.

There is only one word which summarizes this experience, Unreason: all that, for reason, is closest and most remote, emptiest and most complete; all that present itself to reason in familiar structures—authorizing a knowledge, and then a silence, which seeks to be positive—and all that is constantly in retreat from reason, in the inaccessible domain of nothingness (Foucault 101). Further, Foucault assigns a value to classical unreason: "we must understand it not as reason diseased, or as reason lost or alienated, but quite simply as reason dazzled" (101).

He considers madness as a part of everyday experience. The voice of a madman should be heard instead of confining it as it is powerful and can result in creativity. The same has been observed in the case of these poets. Their modes of resistance have given them newer equations and newer self-conceptions. Thus, the importance of schizophrenic decentring cannot be ignored.

Moreover, the ultimate compliance or seeming resignation is a stratagem to survive amidst all kinds of unchanging oppressions and absurdities. Therefore, this compliance is a compliance with a difference. This is the compliance after vital and valid realizations and comprehensions. It is a strategic compliance, a survival tactic, with the potential to result in new equations and newer self-conceptions.

> As psychoanalysis constantly reiterates to us, the difficulty lies in the fact that the human mind does not proceed directly. It does not respond well to radical and immediate change, but repeatedly circumnavigates and exhausts every alternative it already knows until it is satisfied that it is sufficiently bored. (Smith 1)

The schizophrenia in case of these poets is a "put on." This schizophrenia, hence, has been adopted as a mode of resistance—as portent of new emergences, new ways of being, newer consciousness.

Thus, a psychoanalytical study of the similarities and differences of the poets taken up for the study reveals that the conflicts and dualities which the contemporary poets face between passivity and defiance, between the need for domestic security and the desire for independence, between the ways they want to behave and the ways they are made to behave have led to frustrations and sufferings in their life and poetry. Their anguished tortured psyche struggles and their final resignation confirms their so-called schizophrenic existence.

However, in the ultimate analysis, it has been found as Deleuze and Guattari's Anti-Oedipus proves that the desire of these poets does not come from lack and all the efforts made by these poets are not, in vain as in Freudian understanding. On the contrary, desire is a productive force. It is not a theatre, but a factory. It's a productive, real force—and not an imaginary fantasy as psychoanalysis limits it. Though the poets have not achieved too much, yet their embarking upon their quest as women, as poets and as individuals has brought greater self-confidence and awareness among women in general. The dualities and the conflicts in their minds have given them some status and respect in their lives if not equal. They are writing and publishing good verse, evolving tradition both at the thematic and the stylistic level. At the social level they have championed the cause of women with an unparallelled fervour as they have laid bare in literature a feminine world. These poets stand at the threshold of tremendous possibilities today and the future seems to be very promising. Hence, the significance of this schizophrenic decentring as in the case of these poets cannot be overlooked. Newer axis can only emerge if the given axis ruptures into smithereens.

Works Cited

Bajaj, Rashmi. *Women Indo-Anglian Poets: A Critique*. New Delhi: Asian, 1996.

Beauvoir, Simone de. *The Second Sex*. Trans. H.M. Parshley. New York: Vintage, 1952.

de Souza, Eunice, ed. *Nine Indian Women Poets: An Anthology*. New Delhi: Oxford UP, 1997.

Foucault, Michel. *Madness and Civilization: A History of Insanity in the Age of Reason*. Trans. Richard Howard. London: Routledge, 2001.

Graziano, Frank. "Poetry Writing Therapy and Schizophrenia: A Poet's Point of View." *Literature and Psychology* 29.1 (1979): 49-59.

Hasan, Seemin. "Poetry by Women in Post-Independence India." *Re-Markings*. 7.2 (2006): 20-26.

Jain, Sunita. *Sensum: Collected Poems* (1965-2000). New Delhi: Read Books, 2007.

_____. Personal Interview. 30 June 2007.

_____. Interview with Eunice de Souza. *Talking Poems: Conversations with Poets*. New Delhi: Oxford UP, 1999. 57-66.

Kalia, Mamta. Personal Interview. 23 Mar. 2008.

Sahgal, Nayantara. "The Schizophrenic Imagination." *Creative Theory: Writers or Writing*. Ed. Jasbir Jain. Delhi: Pencraft, 2000. 104-11.

Showalter, Elaine. "Feminist Criticism in the Wilderness." *Modern Criticism and Theory*. Ed. David Lodge. Delhi: Pearson Education, 1988. 307-30.

Vijayasree, C. *Suniti Namjoshi: The Artful Transgressor*. Jaipur: Rawat, 2001.

Welleck, Rene, and Austin Warren. "Literature and Psychology." *Theory of Literature*. London: Penguin, 1949.

Smith, Poppi. Abstract. *The Divided Self: A Psychoanalytic Comparison between the Fictional Works of Catharine Lim and Margaret Gibson*. 2005. Nov. 16, 2009 <http:/www.ell.nie.edu.sg/inner Pages/research/ DOP_PS.htm>.